CHAMPIONSHIP OMAHA

- Omaha High-Low
- Pot-Limit Omaha
- Limit High Omaha

T. J. Cloutier
Tom McEvoy

Championship Omaha
Omaha High-Low, Pot-Limit Omaha, Limit High Omaha
by T. J. Cloutier and Tom McEvoy

Copyright 1999 by T. J. Cloutier,
Tom McEvoy and Dana Smith

Library of Congress Catalog Card Number: 98-67030

ISBN: 1-884466-27-3

First Printing: 1999
Second Printing: 2001
Third Printing: 2004

Editor: Dana Smith

Cover Design: Christene King

Cover Photo courtesy of Larry Grossman,
author of *You Can Bet On It!*

Cardsmith Publishing
Poker Plus Publications
4535 W. Sahara, #105
Las Vegas, NV 89102
Fax: (702) 220-4607

e-mail: cardsmith@cox.net

www.pokerbooks.com
e-mail: <author>@pokerbooks.com

TABLE OF CONTENTS

Acknowledgements

Bob Ciaffone, supportive friend and intimidating poker foe, was generous with his time and talent in reading the manuscript and writing the foreword for this book. To the man who so many poker players call "coach," we send our gratitude.

Bob Walker, world-class pot-limit Omaha player, spent many hours reading the rough draft and making valuable suggestions for its improvement. We are indeed grateful for his expert assistance.

Another top player to whom we owe a sincere thank you is Don Vines, who made suggestions for the Omaha high-low chapter and designed several practice hands. We also thank Christene King, who used her creative talents in designing the cover for this book and laying out our advertisements.

Dana Smith, publisher premiere and editor extraordinaire, exercised an incredible degree of patience and perserverance in working with the authors to get this book to press. For her insights and industry, we are deeply grateful. ♣

FOREWORD

by Bob Ciaffone,
World-Class Poker Player &
Author of "Improve Your Poker"

At the start of the third millennium, we find that the amount of information available to us in nearly every area of life is overwhelming. The problem is that quite a bit of it is inferior or incorrect, and the heavy burden of sorting through this large quantity of material to separate the wheat from the chaff, so to speak, is placed upon the information seeker. Just like everyone else, poker players are confronted with this problem. How should a poker player who wishes to improve his game go about it?

I think the most important principle to follow in evaluating the reliability of information is the simple one of considering its source. If you want to gamble on the accuracy of your information, look to an amateur for advice. If you want a high degree of assurance, look to a professional with a proven track record over a long period of time. I think you should adopt this policy whether you intend to speculate in the stock market, mold your golf swing, or improve your poker game.

I have known Tom McEvoy and T. J. Cloutier for many years and am well acquainted with their poker careers. I can certainly vouch for the fact that they have relied on playing poker as the main source of their income for the entire time that I have known them, and that they have achieved high stature in the poker world.

Tom won the title of World Champion at the 1983 World Series Of Poker. Although he plays in both money games and tournaments, he is best-known as a tournament competitor. Tom is one of the most experienced and knowledgable people in the country in the art of poker tournament competition, and has written extensively on that subject.

Recently, he joined forces with T. J. in his writing efforts, and this is the second book produced by that alliance. The reason Tom chose to do this is because T. J. has established himself on the tournament circuit as the most successful player of the last ten years in winning the premier event of major poker tournaments, the grand finale no-limit hold'em competition, which has the largest buy-in amount of any event.

We are all fortunate when someone who is the best in the world at something is willing to put his thoughts on paper for our benefit. Both Tom and T. J. have been successful in winning Omaha events as well, and are greatly experienced at that form of poker. Hence this book.

They have not aimed their work at the novice player, or even someone who knows poker well and now wants to learn how to play Omaha. Rather, a certain degree of familiarity with Omaha on the part of the reader is assumed. This book is for the Omaha player who wants to improve his game. It covers tournament play, pot-limit high Omaha, limit high Omaha, limit Omaha eight-or-better, and even low-stakes play. The authors' style is conversational, in the same manner as their previous work. They tell many stories about poker hands and well-known players, so I am sure that you will be entertained as well as educated.

I have to admit that my own game has been improved by copying a number of plays that I have seen T. J. put on his opponents over the years. Of course, reasonable men may differ in the fine tuning they wish to apply to their poker game, but I can certainly vouch for the fact that T. J. and Tom have enjoyed great success with the ideas they have passed on to you in this book. Anyone can benefit from the top-flight professional advice they dispense. ♣

INTRODUCTION

by Tom McEvoy
1992 World Champion,
Limit High Omaha

Once again I have the pleasure of collaborating with T. J. Cloutier, my friend and world-class poker player, on a poker book. Our first team-written book, Championship No-Limit and Pot-Limit Hold'em, was successful beyond imagination. It has been in steadily increasing demand for the past two years, not only from gambling book stores across the nation but from general book outlets such as Barnes and Noble and Borders Books.

Our success story with the hold'em book has been so gratifying that we decided to write Championship Omaha on the three types of Omaha, games in which we hold four World Series of Poker bracelets between us. In this book T. J. and I tell you some of the strategies we've used to get to the winner's circle in Omaha cash games and tournament events. Our goal is to show you how to get there, too.

In the opening chapter we discuss several basic principles of winning play at any type of Omaha game. Particularly important is the concept of always playing four cards that work together and avoiding hands with "danglers" in them, a word that T. J. coined to describe a card that doesn't work with your other three cards. We expand on this thread of thought throughout the strategy chapters on Omaha high-low, pot-limit Omaha and limit high Omaha.

Omaha high-low has been described by Shane Smith as a game that was invented by a sadist and is played by masochists. T. J., who won the Omaha high-low title at the World

Series in 1994, takes the lead in this chapter, which stresses the importance of hand value and drawing to the nuts.

Pot-limit Omaha is one of the most exciting, big-bet games in poker. At the World Series of Poker in 1998, T. J. overcame terrific opposition at the final table of the pot-limit Omaha event to emerge victorious over such class players as Doyle Brunson and Erik Seidel. In the pot-limit chapter, he explains what you have to do to get the money in this roller-coaster game that is played by many of the world's highest-stakes players.

Since I won the championship in limit high Omaha in 1992, I take the lead in the high Omaha chapter and T. J. adds the commentary. In this chapter we explain how the limit game differs from the pot-limit version and why limit Omaha is not only one of the most volatile games in poker but also is one of the most exciting games for action players.

Chapter Five illustrates twenty-one Omaha hands and describes how T. J. and I would play them in ring games and tournaments. We have included sidegame strategy and tournament tips in each of the game chapters, with some follow-up advice on playing tournaments in Chapter Six.

No book authored by T. J. would be complete without a few of his famous road stories, which you'll find in Chapter Seven, followed by a Glossary of Poker Terms that we use in this book. After all, not everyone may understand what T. J. means when he says, "He was playing a dangler and when the board ragged off on the end he was a gone goose."

We have put our best efforts into the writing of Championship Omaha and sincerely hope that you get as much out of it as we have put into it. After you study the strategies in this book, I'm sure that (as I always close my "Tournament Talk" columns in Card Player magazine), T. J. and I will be seeing you in the winner's circle. ♣

T. J. CLOUTIER
PLAYER OF THE YEAR, 1998

by Dana Smith

T. J. Cloutier is the only player ever to win World Series of Poker championships in all three forms of Omaha poker. He began his string of WSOP victories by winning the limit high Omaha title in 1987. In 1994 he added two bracelets, one in Omaha high-low and the other in pot-limit hold'em. By the time 1998 came along, T. J. was well honed to take the title in pot-limit Omaha, edging out the legendary Doyle Brunson, who finished second.

T. J. is two wrists short of being able to wear all his WSOP bracelets, but if the past is any predictor of the future I'm sure he'll add a few more of them to his jewelry case in the coming years. In fact, he almost won a fifth bracelet for his gold collection in 1998 when he finished third to veteran Scott Nguyen and newcomer Kevin McBride in the championship event. I think you'll enjoy reading his account of that momentous feat — his third appearance in the final six at the Big One — in the tournament chapter of this book.

"1998 Player of the Year" is the latest title T. J. has claimed. He won that distinction by tallying more points for wins and shows than any other tournament player in the United States. Some people think of him as primarily being a hold'em aficionado, but T. J. actually is a very versatile player. "He has demonstrated his mastery of all games," Nolan Dalla wrote in his Card Player report.

In his 1998 tournament play, T. J. ranked among the top ten players in the world in five categories out of six — limit and pot-limit Omaha, Omaha high-low, pot-limit hold'em, limit hold'em, and no-limit hold'em. "T. J. is one of the very best all-around tournament players today," said Jack McClelland.

"At 6'5" and 272 pounds, I'm a *very* well-rounded player!" T. J. laughed, demonstrating a sense of humor toned by just a touch of humility. You see, in addition to his prowess and intimidating qualities in tournament play, T. J. is a very big man in other aspects of his life. He is spontaneous, approachable, sincere ... in short, he has a terrific personality.

"A lot of players can put together a winning tournament record for one or two years," Tom McEvoy explained, "but let's see them do it for 15 years like T. J. has done. The Player of the Year award has been given for only two years, and T. J. was second in 1997 and first in 1998." Mike Sexton has referred to him as "T. J., The Magnificent" and Berry Johnston said, "If there is one player that all of us fear the most at the final table, it is T. J. Cloutier." All of which shows how much respect he has earned from his peers in the world of poker.

"What do you think the great tournament players have in common?" I asked T. J. "I think they're all different," he answered. "What works for me might not work for somebody else. Total concentration and knowing the players — they all have that.

"Some of them are specialists who only play certain events, but I have proved a basic factor to be true, one that I think is integral to tournament success. I seldom play stud eight-or-better, but I recently knocked off a stud/8 tournament. This proves what I've been saying all along — tournament poker is still just tournament poker. If you have a basic knowledge of poker games and you know how to play tournament strategy, you can get there in any tournament game."

With his usual wit, T. J. added, "If I would just stick to poker, I'd be fine. It's all the other fun games that sometimes get to me. The best advice I have for you is to do as I say and not as I do."

To which Tom replied, "I couldn't agree more!" ♣

10

A TRIBUTE TO BENNY

from T. J. Cloutier

I'll never forget Benny Binion's birthday party not long before he died. It was held at Cowboy's in Fort Worth, Texas, a great big Western place with food and drink — it even has a little rodeo arena and a big dance hall where all the best Country bands play.

People came from all over the world to pay tribute to Benny. He hadn't been able to go back to Texas for all those years because he had outstanding charges against him or something like that, but he finally got them quashed. Everybody who's anybody showed up ... Bobby Baldwin, Doyle Brunson ... they all were there. Cowboy's is enormous and it was packed for this tribute to Benny. His family threw the party, and maybe Doyle had something to do with it, too, because they were close friends. Benny's former bodyguard, R. D. Matthews (everybody called him "Patch), probably was in on the party also.

Benny was all decked out for his birthday bash. He always wore Western suits and a beige 20-X Stetson, the best you can buy. He was the type of guy that, if you caught him on a good day — say you got broke and he knew you, and he knew that you gambled in his joint — you could go to him and get a couple of thousand dollars without putting up any security. He'd just flip it to you and say, "Pay it when you can, son." Jack Binion was the same way.

It's funny how we're all connected a little bit. Just after he'd had an aneurysm, Lyle Berman was playing in a tournament at the Horseshoe and fell over in his chair. I took Lyle to the hospital and while we were there, I heard that Benny was in the hospital, too, and so I went up to see him. I've always been thankful that I was able to see him that night, the night before he died. One of his nephews was sitting beside his bed and although Benny couldn't recognize me, at least I could say good-bye to him.

Benny left a legacy to the world of poker. Essentially, what he did by starting the World Series of Poker was to move poker from having a bad taste in the mouth to most of your normal citizens walking around who aren't poker players to making it "legitimate" by putting it into casinos. Amarillo Slim had a lot to do with that, too. For all his flamboyance and the way he talks on TV and all that stuff, Slim has done a lot for poker. But mainly it was Benny — the World Series of Poker is what started it all and we owe a big debt of gratitude to him for that. How do you replace a guy like Benny? You don't.

What poker players can do now to improve the reputation of poker is to stop acting like idiots, quit throwing cards and getting up and stomping around the poker table when they take a beat. If they don't clean up their act, poker will end up right back where it started, in the backroom, because people aren't going to continue putting up with that kind of stuff. Benny helped bring it out of the backrooms and if we don't guard that legacy it's going to go back to where it started.

I mean, in the old days if somebody asked you what you did for a profession, if you were a poker player you told them that you were in investments, right? Or I do this, or I do that. Nowadays if they ask you what you do for a living, you can just say, "I play poker." That's a big difference.

And we owe it all to Benny. ♣

12

Chapter One

GENERAL PRINCIPLES FOR WINNING AT OMAHA

by T. J. Cloutier
Commentary by Tom McEvoy

One of the most important things to understand about Omaha poker is that all forms of Omaha are hand-value driven games. That is, the starting value of hands is usually paramount to position, which is far less important in Omaha than it is in limit or pot-limit hold'em.

You should always start with four related cards that work together in some way. On the flop you should have either the best hand possible or a draw to it in order to continue with the hand. If you have a drawing hand, you should have a draw that will win the pot if you make it. When you draw for flushes, draw for the nut flush. When you draw for straights, draw for the nut straight. In other words, you should only be drawing to the nuts.

The Best Draw with Backup

This is a concept that is important in ring games and is *really* important in tournaments: If you have a drawing hand, you should have a backup to your draw, a secondary draw. For example, in Omaha high-low you might flop top set and also have a low draw or even a three-flush for backup. In high Omaha, you might flop the top set or second set, plus a draw at the nut flush or the nut straight to go with it. With your backup draw(s), you have a lot more ways to make the hand stand up than if you only had a set.

Now let's say that you're playing a pot-limit Omaha tournament and make a set on the flop with no straight or flush possibilities in your hand (no backup draw). If either a flush or straight card comes on fourth street, are you going to call a big bet to try to pair the board on the end? You really have to watch yourself in these situations in tournaments, where having a backup draw is so important.

Pot-limit Omaha is the only game ever devised in which you can flop the nuts and have to throw it away on the flop! Suppose you flop the nut straight and you get action on it. If there are two suited cards out there and you get more than one-way action on the hand, it means that someone probably has a set and someone else most likely has a nut-flush draw — you're a dog in this hand.

That's the difference between pot-limit and limit Omaha. In limit Omaha where it costs only a one-unit bet, you have to play the hand and hope that nobody draws out on you. But in pot-limit Omaha you'll have to stand all that money and then pray that the hand holds up, so quite often the best thing to do is to dump it. All top tournament players have done that a zillion times.

How about a draw to the nut flush in pot-limit Omaha with no backup? For a lot of money, I think it would be a bad call, especially heads-up. Don't get me wrong: If you're getting big odds on your money it may be different. Sometimes there's a lot of money in the pot before the flop and you're getting three or four-way action. In that case if you flop the nut flush draw with all of the action *in front* of you, you might want to continue. But you don't want to be the first man to act with this hand — you have to check it from up front because all you have is a draw.

Now let's say that you're in a ring game and there's action in front of you. Then you almost have to call the bet if you're in a big pot and *if* you're willing to go to your pocket again. But in a tournament (unless you're short-stacked and just trying to get a hold of some chips) you simply couldn't call a bet because if you lose you're out of the tournament.

You can play a lot more hands after the flop in limit Omaha than in pot-limit. That's the difference between the two: You might take a draw in a limit game that you would not take in either a pot-limit game or a tournament. But in both games, it's always nice to have a backup draw.

The Danger of the Dangler

A lot of people play hands that I call "three cards with a dangler." Say that you have K-Q-J-2. Obviously, the deuce doesn't fit with anything else — it's a dangler. But you see a lot of people playing these types of hands, even a lot of good players in big games. They know they have the three big cards that they can make straights with or big full houses or high sets, so they discount the value of having a fourth connecting card. As for me, I can't do that. I won't play a dangler hand like K-Q-J-2, even if the king happens to be suited, because you never have the nut flush draw with it.

"You want four cards that interact with each other in some fashion," Tom adds. "The times when you might consider playing a three-card hand usually are in unraised pots, late position (on or next to the button), and when three of your cards are fairly strong. You virtually never play one from up front unless you happen to be in the big or small blinds.

"But let's face it: We're talking Omaha here! A lot of people play a lot of hands and they don't always have four cards that interact ... they slip in with three-card hands." Yes, and a lot of times they slip right out of the game busted.

The Dual Nature of Omaha High-Low

Remember that Omaha high-low is a two-tiered game: You play big hands or you play little hands. You do not play middle hands. You play Omaha high-low as though you were playing with a stripped deck, as though the sevens, eights and nines weren't in the deck. You say to yourself, "I can't win playing sevens, eights and nines in this game."

For the number of times that you will win pots with middle hands, you'll get eaten alive in the long run. Big hands are big pairs with connectors and big rundowns, and little hands are those with little rundowns that include an ace. A pair of aces with a deuce-trey is both big and little — you like this hand because you usually can't get counterfeited for low with it — and you like two aces with a deuce and some other low card. These are the types of hands to play.

Any time you're playing Omaha high-low, you want to have an ace in your hand, unlike pot-limit Omaha in which four connected cards or hands like 7-7-6-5 are playing hands, especially in unraised pots. The middle cards have a lot of value in high Omaha but almost no value in Omaha high-low. The main difference between the hands that you play in high Omaha (including pot-limit) and the ones you play in Omaha high-low is that you play the middle cards in the high games and you don't play them in high-low.

Strong Hands in Omaha High-Low

Everybody knows that the best hand in Omaha high-low is A-A-2-3 double-suited. Then it progresses to A-A-2-4 or A-A-2-5 (two aces with two wheel cards). After these hands come the rundown hands such as A-2-3-4 with the ace suited. An A-K-2-3 double-suited is also a powerful hand, but it comes further down the line in strength. The value of having an ace with three wheel cards is that you'll rarely get counterfeited for the low.

I've seen a lot of players play hands with only three related cards — for example, they come into a high Omaha pot with A-K-Q-6. I think those are "sucker hands." However, if the A-6 is suited, it's different because then you also have a nut flush draw. In Omaha games you never want to be drawing at the second-nut flush (or the second-nut *anything*, for that matter) because if someone is drawing at a higher flush, making the flush could cost you a lot of money. If your opponent bets, what do you do with the hand?

Strong Hands in High Omaha

In computer runs of the ranking of Omaha hands where your percentage of wins with one particular hand is computed against other hands, the computer comes up with A-A-K-K double-suited as being the best possible starting hand in high Omaha. I thoroughly disagree with the computer on that one.

I think the best possible hand you can start with in high Omaha is A-A-J-10 double-suited. Obviously, you can make more straights with this hand than you can with A-A-K-K double-suited. Naturally, you can't make three kings with the A-A-J-10 but the only thing that having two kings in your hand does for you is give you the possibility of making three kings (or four kings). The A-A-J-10 nullifies the power of the kings by having that many more hands you can draw to that will be nut hands if you make them.

If the flop comes with a K-Q, you have a wraparound straight draw and an overpair. If it comes 7-8-9 you have the nuts with the J-10. If it comes with an 8-9, you have a great top-wrap with the aces also working. In fact, every straight that you can make with the J-10 and the two aces are nut hands. And you still have the possibility of making the nut flush in either of your suits.

Plus, look at what happens when the flop comes J-J-X or 10-10-X. You have top set with top kicker working for you (and an overpair). And a lot of times, a small pair will come on the board and then you have a chance of winning the pot with aces-up. With a flop such as 7-7-2, for example, you might win with aces and sevens. Therefore, as far as I'm concerned, the number-one hand in both limit and pot-limit Omaha is A-A-J-10 double-suited.

Knowing Your Opponents

As in every other form of poker, you have to know the players in your Omaha game. Who will raise with bare aces before the flop without any suits in high Omaha? Who won't? Who will only raise with aces double-suited? (And there are a lot of players like that.) Or who will only raise with A-K-Q-J double-suited? Or with A-A-2-3 in Omaha high-low? You must know who those players are.

I've won a lot of money in pot-limit Omaha cash games and tournaments where it didn't cost me very much to call the raise in situations in which I could definitely put both of my opponents on aces. When I know their aces are gone, I might play a hand such as 4-5-6-7 because I stand to win a big pot if I make the hand. I don't necessarily need this type of hand to be suited because I'd have to give them credit for having suits, although as Tom points out, it's still better to be suited than unsuited. Hands like 5-6-7-7 or 5-5-6-7 or 5-6-6-7 — any of those types of hands in which you have three rundown cards with a pair — will take the aces right off a lot of times.

But here's the deciding factor in whether you play this type of hand: You must know in advance that both opponents are playing aces. And you don't want to see a pair on the board ... you never want to see a pair come on the board in that situation unless it makes a set for you because your opponents could win the hand with aces up.

Your opponents will "show" you what they're playing. Suppose one guy raises and the next guy reraises. You know that the first guy will only raise with aces and you know that if the second guy reraises he has aces for sure — because in pot-limit Omaha nobody reraises unless he has aces (except for certain maniacs who will raise or reraise with any four cards that are double-suited). In a ring game especially, if you have a hand like the ones I've mentioned, it's worth calling because you have a chance to win some big money. Your opponents have already put in a lot of money and if they get a small flop, they're coming with it. You won't have to lead to them — they're going to bet it for you! And this is exactly what you're looking for. In every pot-limit Omaha tournament in which I've done well, at some point I've had a rundown hand with a pair against two people with aces (or one opponent with aces and the other one with kings), caught a small or medium flop and taken them off their hands.

Tom gives an example from an Omaha high-low game: "I was playing in a $20-$40 Omaha high-low game with a kill pot. I had to put in a $20 forced bet and I had the button. Fred, who would never get out of line (he's the type of player that T. J. calls a "supernit"), raises from first position and gets called by one other player. I know that Fred has either an A-2 with two little cards working, or an A-2 with a big pair, or aces with two face cards — one of these three hands. I have a 10-9-7-6 with $20 already in the pot. I knew exactly where Fred was at although the other guy's hand was a bit questionable. So, I decided to call $20 more.

"The flop came J-8-8, three different suits. Fred came out betting and the second player folded. You know what my play was? I raised. He thought about it for a few seconds and mucked his hand, showing it to me first. He had A-2-Q-Q with one suit."

Playing Against Tight Players

The "nit" that Tom mentions is a player who plays too tight, taking no chances. Here's an example of what makes Fred a "supernit." He will drive from one county to the other, win one pot, quit the game and drive home. He might drive 100 miles to win that one pot — now to me, that is a supernit! When he sits down, you know that he's not going to play for long unless he gets stuck. All the nits are the same way: When they're stuck, all bets are off, but if they can win one pot they're out of there. I actually saw this supernit get loser in a game, make a comeback to $50 winner, and quit the game — all within thirty minutes!

Supernits may know all the odds but there's no gamble to them. When they play in the tournaments and it gets down to the last tables, I purposely shoot at them because I know that when I make a move, if they don't have two aces, I'll win the pot. If they put money into the pot, I'm coming over the top of them, though not necessarily before the flop.

Against a particularly tight player in a tournament a few years ago, I knew that I could steal the pot from him if the flop came bad for him. I must've taken the pot away from him seven or eight times in that tournament and never at any time did I have a hand! This is the type of thing that you can do against supernits. I know that if a supernit raises the pot and I reraise him, he figures that if he has jacks, for example, I must have him beat. And *I* know that *he* knows that, so I'm raising him with almost anything.

"Somebody once said that T. J. sits like a coiled cobra in the corner of a room waiting to strike," Tom adds. "When I first heard that, I thought of a cartoon I had seen in which two vultures are perched on a bluff overlooking the road. One says to the other, 'To hell with waiting any longer, I'm gonna go kill something!'

"That's T. J.'s style, picking his victims by swooping down on them. He has enough nerve to make a play against a known tight player who he knows has a decent starting hand. Not everybody can get away with that."

The difference between players with natural instincts and those who do not have innate ability at poker is that none of the moves that more advanced players make come naturally to them. They have to sit there and think about each play. After thinking it through, they often make a "long" call (when you take a long time to make a decision). If you take a long time to make a move, your opponents have plenty of time to think about what you're doing and figure out what they are going to do after you make your move. But if you do everything in the flow of the game, things go more smoothly for you because your opponents don't have time to analyze what you're doing. This is why things flow for people who have natural talent. Poker books are good instructional tools to get you up to speed when you're new to a game, and they certainly help a lot of players, but you still have to develop your own personal style. We hope that learning the concepts in this book will help you develop a winning style and give you the knowledge you need to play with confidence.

Getting into the Flow

Someone has suggested that you should keep asking yourself questions like, "If I make my hand, will it be the nuts?" That's fine for new players, but I think that after you've been playing for a while things should start coming naturally to you. The answers to these questions are things that you should already know — it should all come to you in the flow of the game. You shouldn't have to hem and haw around and say, "Well, if this card comes I'm okay but if that card comes I'm in bad shape." Until you can play any poker game and maintain an even pace, you'll never be successful at it. (I hope that you will be able to maintain a more even flow in your game after you've read this book.)

I never take any time on any hand, period, I don't care what game it is. I always do things at a particular pace that is natural for the way that I play cards. Good players are going to read you — they know how to read their opponents — but if you're in a steady flow all the time, they can't read a thing. They may think they know something, but they don't know it for sure.

In bridge, you have to think three or four tricks ahead in the play. You have to learn to play poker in the same way — it should all be in your mind that if this card comes, I can do this; and if that card comes, I can do that; and if the rest of them come, I can't do anything — so that when the cards come on the flop, you can move right away. You're always playing ahead of yourself. "Right after the flop, you should know how you're going to play the entire hand depending on what slips off the deck after the flop" is the way Tom puts it.

Raising in Pot-Limit Omaha

The man that I consider to be the best high-stakes Omaha player alive is Lyle Berman. I think he has the best mind for the game. He once told me that in any pot-limit Omaha tournament, there is no hand worth putting in the first raise before the flop. I'm not saying that he suggested that you don't *reraise* with aces double-suited to knock the field down to one player if you can — of course, you can do that. But you seldom put in the *first* raise with *any* hand. When you think about it, do you know how often players get broke in tournaments and side games with two aces?! An enormous amount of times.

You see, that first raise is never big enough to shut people out. They know where you're at most of the time. That's why I might make a raise in a ring game with a 10-10-9-8, for example, from around back. I *want* them to put me on aces. And then I want to flop middle cards and see what happens.

What Lyle said is so true it's pitiful: If anybody has a decent playing hand, he's going to call the first raise at least. You can't knock anybody out with the first raise anyhow, so let *them* do the raising. If you want to do something in pot-limit Omaha, look for a situation like the following: There are three players in the pot, somebody raises and then gets called in two spots. By this time there's enough money in the pot that you can either shut out all of them or all except one of them with a pot-sized reraise. You see, the pot has to be big enough in pot-limit to allow you to put in enough money to shut out the other players. This is why I believe that Lyle's theory is so right: There is no hand strong enough for a good player to make the first raise in pot-limit Omaha.

Raising in Omaha High-Low

"Hal Kant gave me a piece of advice for Omaha high-low," Tom says. "He suggested that when you have four premium low cards in your hand (such as A-2-4-5) you should not bring it in for a raise because you want as many players as possible to come into the pot with you. They won't be expecting you to have that strong a hand in an unraised pot."

In Omaha high-low, you're going to get played with most of the time because it's a limit-structure game; because of that, there usually are a lot of players in every pot. When you raise before the flop, you're tipping the strength of your hand. I'm not saying that you *never* raise before the flop in Omaha high-low: In fact, I probably raise more before the flop in that game than I ever would raise in pot-limit Omaha because in Omaha high-low, it costs only one unit to raise so it doesn't cost you all that much. If you don't flop to it, you can get away from the hand anyway, so it's cheap.

The purpose of the raise in Omaha high-low is to build the pot, not to limit the field. You can hardly eliminate anybody because if someone is going to play the hand, he'll call at least one raise. When you come in with premium cards, you're hoping to induce somebody with a hand such as K-Q-2-3 to play with you. (As far as I'm concerned, a K-Q-2-3 is just sucker bait. You have no nut-flush draws and if there's any action before the flop, you know that the aces are gone so you're not likely to catch your key card, an ace.)

Look for the Right Situation

There are marginal hands, even in a tournament, that you can play in exactly the right situations. For example, suppose only one guy has called the pot in Omaha high-low and you're around back with 2-3-4-5 where you don't figure to get raised. This isn't a super strong hand, but in this situation you can play it. You're hoping to catch an ace or make a straight to win the high end, or you might even have the best low against only one player. At least you know that an ace probably is available because there's been no action before the flop.

Since it costs you just one limit bet, you can call. Then if an ace and another low card come on the flop, you're in hog heaven. If you catch the ace and another little card that pairs one of yours, you have a pair, yes, but you have the wheel draw and a low going for you with the chance for a scooper.

However, if three or four people have come into the pot in front of you, that 2-3-4-5 is nothing. It's a piece of cheese because the aces are already busy. Suppose the flop comes with 8-6-3. You have a straight draw, yes, but you know the aces are busy so you can't have the nut low unless an ace hits the board. And only a deuce will give you the nut straight — any other straight that you make won't be the nuts, so you can get into further trouble. This hand is *el trappo maximus*.

You have to think about all of these things when you're playing Omaha high-low, especially in a multiway pot in late position when it looks like the aces are gone. If four players are in there with you, you can just about bank on two of the aces being busy.

The reason that Omaha high-low is so popular these days is that so many people don't know what hands to play and the good players take advantage of that. The good players will beat these bad players to death. If the flop comes K-9-3 and the bad player has four little cards in his hand, he'll stay in to see fourth street. It seems that fourth street invariably gives him another low card so that he can justify calling another bet. Then it rags on the end and he's a gone goose for all the money he's put in the pot. He will remember the one time he made a hand like that and not the ten times he lost to it. Tom calls this "selective memory."

Straights in Limit High and Pot-Limit Omaha

You will play situations in limit high Omaha that you would never consider playing in pot-limit Omaha. You will stand raises with more borderline hands in limit than you ever will in pot-limit. If you flop the nut straight in limit high Omaha, you'll play it even if there are two suited cards along with it, but in pot-limit you might find yourself folding it on the flop if there's any action. Of course, you might play it in pot-limit Omaha if three suits come on the flop. If you flop the nut straight in this scenario and someone gives you action, he probably has a set because there obviously is no flush draw on the board. In this case, you're favored over his pairing the board or catching a running pair, so now you can play the hand.

The point is that in limit high Omaha you'll play your nut straight on the flop even with two suited cards on the board because it's only costing you one unit at a time. But in pot-limit Omaha it can cost you your whole stack at any time once there's money in the pot. So, one of the basic differences between the two is your selection of which hands you play on the flop.

The Role of Position

Position is a much stronger consideration in pot-limit than it is in limit high Omaha or Omaha high-low. In the limit games you know that people are calling bets to their draws and that they will call again on fourth street — but they don't do that in pot-limit because it costs them too much money to draw. Basically, the major difference between limit high and pot-limit Omaha is how many times you'll get to fifth street in the limit version compared to how many times you'll get there in pot-limit.

And there usually are more multiway pots in limit high Omaha, whereas in pot-limit games it's more likely to be heads up or three players at the most (I've never seen four people go to the river in a big raised pot in a pot-limit game). As Tom puts it, "Either hitting the flop or hitting a draw to the nuts is more important in pot-limit than it is in limit."

Reading the Board

I've seen a great many low-limit players misread the board, especially in Omaha high-low. Where novice players seem to get mixed up most often is when a set comes on the board. They don't have a pair in their hand but they have an ace and there's an ace on the board. They forget that they have to play two cards from their hand and that if they don't have a pair in their hand, they don't have a full house. Of the mistakes I've seen people make in Omaha, that is the biggest one. (We used to play a game called Fort Worth hold'em in which you had to play both cards out of your hand. Boy, if you want to see hold'em players mess up when there are trips on the board, try this game!)

Another big mistake that Omaha high-low players make is not reading their hand correctly when they get counterfeited for low. A player might have an A-2-4-7 in his hand, for example, and A-5-8 comes on the board. Since the ace is showing on the board, he thinks he's been counterfeited. As simple a mistake as this is, it is very common. I think that people who have problems reading the board should practice at home with difficult flops that counterfeit the low or show sets, and so on.

Top and Bottom Pair

Flopping top and bottom pair can be fine if you're against one person, but it's really not the hand to be betting against more than one opponent in Omaha. And for sure, you don't want to be playing the bottom two pair. The bottom two pair in any form of Omaha is death and destruction.

Suppose you're playing in a limit high Omaha game with that dangler hand, the K-Q-J-2, and the flop comes K-8-2. You've flopped kings and deuces, top and bottom pair. If someone bets, you call, and there's a raise behind you, there's a pretty good chance you're up against three of a kind, or kings and eights at the least. You're in trouble.

Even if you're playing a hand with a pair in it and flop bottom set, you'd better be prepared to throw it away against any action. "This is why the small pairs can get you into a world of hurt when you flop a set to them" observes Tom. "There are a lot more sets out in Omaha than in other games. Set over set, which is relatively rare in hold'em, is a common occurrence in Omaha games. If you're playing pot-limit for big numbers, you really don't want to lead at the pot with bottom set."

Decision Hands

Great hands play themselves and terrible hands play themselves. It is how you play the in-between hands that can make you or break you in poker. Tom explains it this way: "Decision hands are the bread and butter hands of the pros. It is the bread-and-butter decisions that separate the winning pros from the 'wannabes.' Anybody can play powerful hands or powerful flops and win pots. And most players can recognize trash hands and get away from them cheaply. It is the decisions that you make about all of the in-between hands that separate the men from the boys, the women from the girls, in the poker world. And that's where you win or lose most of your money. "You can have a great winning session just by having the deck hit you in the face, or a losing session when you don't catch any cards at all. And you can lose when you have good cards but run into someone with better cards, like when you flop set over set and you have the worst set, or when you have all your money in on a set or top two-pair and someone hits a flush at the river and takes you off, or when you have the flush and someone fills on the end. This is why losing players have winning sessions sometimes against very strong professional-level winning players. But that's what keeps the lesser-skilled players coming back.

"In all forms of poker, you are rewarded for making correct decisions over the long run. It is all of the marginal, in-between hands that are played with great ability that separate winners from losers. It's what you do when you flop top two pair (which can be a very marginal holding in Omaha) — knowing when the hand is good and when to push it to increase your chances of its holding up, and knowing when to get loose from it.

"For example, say that you have a king-high flush draw, the second-nut flush draw, and your intuition tells you that you're up against the nut flush draw. A strong player will get away from the hand but the weak players can't resist drawing to the second nuts. And when they get there with it, they lose even more money.

"You've heard about the farmer who lost three farms by drawing to inside straights and missing? Then he lost the fourth farm when he drew to one and hit it. The same adage applies to Omaha. Consistently failing to draw to only the nuts or failing to recognize when your draw is less than the nuts but is still the best draw ... that is where the skill comes in. Knowing when that king-high flush draw is the best flush draw out there and that if you hit it, maybe a queen-high flush draw will pay you off — that takes great skill. Or knowing that you have the best hand with two pair and taking measures to protect it that will force people out of the pot. It is these kinds of decisions that make your long-term profit.

"Our editor says that it seems as though the weak player only remembers the time when he made the hand. That's true: Losing players have selective memory. They forget all the times that (a) they didn't make it, or (b) they made it and still lost with it. Omaha is a very volatile game, which means that weak players can play a lot of cards and might catch enough cards or backdoor enough hands on a given day to have a very successful individual winning session. But loose play almost guarantees long-term, disastrous results, *losing* results."

Going On Tilt

Let me tell you a story about one of the worst beats I've seen happen in a tournament. In the no-limit hold'em championship event at the Rio, John Bonetti flopped a set of jacks and Milt Meyers flopped a set of fives. They got all their money in on the flop. At the river Meyers caught a one-outer, the case five, to knock Bonetti out of the tournament.

It's pretty easy for players to go on tilt when things like this happen to them. Everybody who's ever played poker has gone on tilt at some time or other. The idea is to learn from it — if you've gone on tilt ten times, don't make it eleven.

To me, the easiest thing in the world to do is to be loser in a poker game and get up and walk away at a certain point. You can almost count on one hand the times that I've gone off for a big number in a poker game. When I say a big number I mean something like when you buy in for $5,000 and lose it and then put up another $5,000 and lose that. Then you just have to say, "It's not my day, they'll be playing again tomorrow" and walk away.

I've always set a loss limit. I know that some experts say that, whether you're winning or losing, you should stay in a game if you're playing well and the game's good. My theory is that there's almost always a game the next day. I play well enough that I can overcome a $10,000 loss, but what if I get $30,000 into this game and the game the next day isn't going to be that big? Sometimes, big games are random occurrences — they start off as little games and build into big ones. So, if I take a $30,000 loss I might have to wait two months before I can get into a game where I can get that money back. Have I worked playing a smaller game for two months to earn $30,000 and then blow it in one game? That just does not make sense, yet people do it all the time.

I know a player who would go for every dime he had in every poker game he ever played. Doyle and Chip and those guys go for big numbers sometimes, but they have a lot of money ... I mean, a *lot* of money. But as much money as Lyle has and as high as he plays, when he gets to a point he quits. For Lyle, it isn't a question of whether he's going to play the next day because he only has certain days when he can play ... but he still quits.

The Importance of Attitude

It doesn't matter what the game is, you should have a good attitude when you sit down and know that you can play your best. Just *make* yourself play your best. If you have an inclination to do something that you know you shouldn't do, go with your instincts not to do it.

I always say that the things we know, our instincts, are born from what we've learned over the years. Your first instinct is probably going to be right a great percentage of the time. But if you sit there like what we used to call the "gooses," and find out a way that you could possibly have the best hand — put your opponents on a hand that you can beat — you're a fool and have no chance at winning at poker. Maybe there's an ace and a king on the board and you have two eights in your hand and you think, "Well, he might have two sevens so I'm going to call him." If you're thinking this way, you'd better quit playing poker and find a different profession. We used to have an old saying, "Keep your day job."

"We still have that saying!" Tom adds.

Concluding Remarks

Now that we've covered a few general principles of winning at Omaha, Tom and I will discuss some specific pointers on how to win at each type of Omaha. We have included both cash game strategies and tournament techniques in the chapters on Omaha high-low, pot-limit Omaha and limit high Omaha. Then we will show you several practice hands that regularly come up in Omaha and give you our opinions on how to profitably play them in all three types of Omaha.

Our goal in this book is to give you the best advice possible so that you can become a consistent winner at any form of Omaha. Or as our publisher's motto for this series of books goes: "Let the champions lead you to the winners circle." ♣

Chapter 2

OMAHA HIGH-LOW

by T. J. Cloutier,
Commentary by Tom McEvoy
Questions by Dana Smith

In this chapter Tom and Dana and I have three-way conversations about the play of actual Omaha high-low hands in which she asks us about the best strategies in certain situations. Since she plays low-limit tournaments and cash games and Tom and I play the higher limits, you should be able to gain some insights on how Omaha high-low is played differently at various limits in ring games and tournaments.

People think of Omaha high-low as a relatively new game, but we were playing it in Texas in the '70s so it's been around a lot longer than most people know. It's a game that pulls in weak players like no other. A lot of people who are playing it today in the casinos have no idea about which hands to play or their odds of scooping a pot. That's one reason why there are so many multiway pots with as many as nine players in the low-limit games. Dana wrote that Omaha high-low is a game invented by a sadist and played by masochists, and I think there may be a grain of truth in that!

This is a hand-value driven game. Just like other four-card hold'em games, you should not be entering pots unless all four of your cards work together in some way. You usually don't want to play a hand with three good cards and a "dangler" in it because that dangler, the one card that doesn't fit in with the rest of them, can put you in a world of misery. Remember the word *dangler* because you'll be seeing it a lot in this book.

The Low Starting Hands

The best hand is A-A-2-3 double suited. Then comes an A-A-2-3 with one suit and A-A-2-3 with no suit. After these hands come A-A-2-4, A-A-2-5, and so on. Then an A-2-3-4, A-2-3-5, and so on. A-2-3-K or A-2-3-Q suited are great hands, too. The really good players will always have the ace suited when they're playing any kind of decent sized pot.

These low hands rate higher than hands like A-A-K-Q or other premium high hands. A hand such as A-2-K-Q is a good hand but it's one that can get counterfeited very easily. You should always have a third low card to help out against getting counterfeited.

Remember that if you have a hand like A-2-3-4 it can only cost you the original bet or raise before the flop because if the flop comes with high cards, your A-2-3-4 is easy to get away from so you get rid of it. Plus, it cannot get counterfeited for low (unless you make four pair ... and I've had that happen, too). But hands like A-2-3-K or A-2-4-Q are harder to get away from and with certain types of flops, you can really get involved with them. For example, suppose you have:

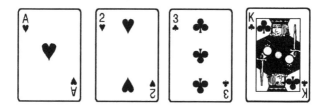

The flop comes:

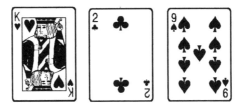

Now you have top and bottom pair and you'll have a nut-low draw if a little card comes on the turn. Things appear to be looking good so you continue with the hand. Then it comes 8♣ 9♥ on the turn and river or 10♥ 10♣ or J♦ 10♦. Then what do you have? You've been involved in the hand because of your two pair on the flop and the nut-low draw you picked up on the turn, and on the end you have nothing!

A Tip From the Top
Don't chase a low on the flop
when it comes with two high cards.

Weak players with good hands like A-2-3-4 will see the flop come with K-J-5 and they'll call the first bet trying to catch a low card. They get involved with the pot, maybe catch another low card on the turn, and then see another high card come or the board pair on the end, and wind up with nothing. That's the difference between a good player and a bad one: The good player won't do that. When a good player has a low hand, he will seldom chase unless at least two low cards come on the flop.

Raising Before the Flop

You have to start with your premium low hands but you also must be careful with them. Ace-deuce alone is not a raising hand. But as Tom observes, "A lot of players who get those premium low starting hands such as A-2-3-4 in early position like to raise with them rather than just call to disguise the strength of their hand and entice weaker hands to come in after them. Hal Kant suggested to me that rather than raise with your premium low hands, you should wait to make your profit on the later streets." He's right. You usually should limp with them.

I think that there are very few occasions when you should raise from early position with *any* hand before the flop in Omaha high-low. Even if you have A-A-2-3 double-suited, I don't believe that you should raise the pot in most games. Of course in a loose, ram-and-jam game where everybody's raising with everything, you can raise with this hand because the chances are good that you will get called in several spots. Usually, however, you don't want to tip your hand; you want to disguise its strength because you want a lot of other players to call and a raise might run four or five players out of the pot who normally would have come into it. You want them in the pot because if you get a good flop to your hand, you can really make some good money with it.

However if you're sitting around back and a couple of people already have come into the pot, that's a different story — if you have A-2-3-4 with the ace suited, you should raise the pot before the flop. If the players in front of you have called one bet, the chances are good that they also will call the raise.

A player once asked me, "In a hold'em game, what if the pot was raised in first position and there were tens, jacks, and queens out and you had two aces. Would you play the hand?" I answered, "In a New York minute! There's no action in hold'em where I wouldn't play or raise with two aces before the flop. Laying it down would be stupid."

But in Omaha high-low, I wouldn't ordinarily raise *from up front* with an A-A-2-3. However, from around back, I don't care what the action has been in front of me, even if it's been raised and reraised, I would put in another reraise with that same A-A-2-3. If you have the best hand that you can possibly get before the flop, why wouldn't you raise with it? In late position, that is.

However, if you have an A-2-8-9, why get heavily involved? Just to get a miracle flop? So the flop comes 5-6-7 and now you have the nut low and the nut high ... but how many times do you get that flop versus how many times the hand costs you money?

A Tip From the Top
In your low hands, you want an A-2 or A-3 with another low card for backup

Remember that you always want a hand with an A-2 or an A-3 in it and at least one other low card. Anytime you can get an A-2 with two other low cards, that's fabulous. Even if you have A-2-6-8, you're going to play the hand. Actually, having the 2-6 to go along with your ace is stronger than you might think. You'll need a 3-4-5 on board to make the wheel and with the A-2-6, you'll have the wheel *and* the six-high straight.

The High Rundown Hands

In my opinion, you should only play big cards when you have a hand like K-Q-J-10 or A-K-Q-J, or a big pair with connectors such as A-A-K-Q or K-K-Q-J — *and* you always want at least one suit. You should *never* play a hand with a dangler — Q-J-10-5 or K-J-10-3, for example. That five and that three are classic examples of danglers.

Key Concept. When you play four high or semi-high straight cards, you always want to have two cards that can make a straight to the ace, so you at least need to have a J-10 in the hand. If you have a Q-J-10-8, for example, at least you have a shot at the high if an ace and any other high card come on the board. And you have a shot at getting some action on the hand because when an ace comes on the flop, somebody usually will have low cards to go with it or will make a pair of aces. The key is that when you play any four straight cards, you always want some part of the rundown to connect with an ace.

Q-J-10-8 isn't necessarily a hand that I recommend playing, but if you're in late position and it's a multiway pot, a lot of your opponents are usually going to have the low cards. As long as your cards can connect with an ace, you're in jockeying position to win either the high end or possibly scoop the whole pot if an ace comes on the board and a third low card doesn't come. You want the ace on the board because without it you're not going to get any action on the hand.

If you're in late position and there has been a lot of preflop action, you can be pretty sure that two or three aces are out. But if just one ace pops up on the flop, you can be pretty sure that at least one of your opponents has made a pair of aces, two pair or has a low draw, and you will have a pretty good shot at scooping with a high straight.

A Tip from the Top
If there is a lot of preflop action, two or three aces are probably out.

A lot of people play hands with any ace-deuce and random cards. When an ace comes on the flop, it sometimes will change their position from playing a low hand to playing a high hand. For example, they might flop two pair, but you might flop a hand that could destroy them if it comes with an ace and one other high card that connects. You're not going to draw at a middle buster (an inside straight) in this situation because that would be ridiculous. For example, if the flop comes A-10-4, and you have the Q-J-10-8, you're not going to draw for a king. But if it comes A-K-4, you have a good chance at scooping the pot if you catch a queen, jack or ten.

Most pots that are scooped are not won by somebody who is going both ways, they're won by either a high hand or a wheel. The things we've been discussing here are just little things that come up outside the realm of "normal" Omaha high-low hands.

Obviously, you would prefer having an ace in your high rundown hand. When an ace hits the board along with another big card, you have the wrap. Then you play the hand as though you were playing high Omaha, and you hope the little cards don't come because you want to scoop the pot.

Having a big pair in your hand *with* connecting high cards can be important, too. You might flop trips to it and they often will be the top set. You don't want to flop middle or bottom trips where someone might have higher trips than yours and you get tied into the pot. In a high hand other than the rundowns headed by an ace or king, I want to have a big pair ... but I don't want them to be jacks.

Two aces, kings, or queens with connecting big cards are fine and I'll play them, of course, but having two jacks is bad because there are three cards higher than the jack and if someone flops a bigger set than you, you're in trouble. This is why I consider K-Q-J-J to be a very marginal high hand in Omaha high-low. It looks pretty with all that color in it, but it could turn into a big trap for you if the flop comes with something like K-J-4 and there's a lot of action. You could really be hurting against a flop like that. Somebody could have the wrap going and somebody else could have three kings, so you're an underdog. Your only out may be the case jack!

The Big-Pair Hands

I'm not too enthralled with hands that have two big pair in them. Say that you have K-K-9-9. You almost have to flop a set to continue past the flop, and who says a set will win? And how many other hands can you make with two big pair in your hand? At the World Series of Poker you won't find many players who come in with those hands, although in the lower buy-in tournaments (up to $200) you're going to find a multitude of players who will play them. They get in cheap, they don't really know how to play well but they *want* to play, they want to get action — and they're going to destroy a lot of good players. They have no chance of winning the tournament themselves, but they sometimes knock out people who do have a chance of winning it. You can't let it get you down when somebody knocks you out of a tournament playing a hand they shouldn't have played. Without these types of players, nobody would win any amount of money, so sometimes you just have to take your medicine.

Aces and Spaces

Aces with spaces (no connecting cards) are one-way hands. Suppose you have an A-A-9-6 with no suits and there's a raise in front of you. Other than flopping an ace, the only way you probably could win with this hand is if the board comes with a pair (such as tens) and you make aces-up *and* nobody has a set of tens or fills. Always have it in your mind that somebody's in the pot playing those low cards that can make straights and scoop the pot. A-6 is *not* a good low draw!

"People with just average skills usually will play any two aces," adds Tom, "but folding in this scenario is the correct thing to do, especially in a tournament. However, suppose you're in a situation where you know you'll be playing heads-up against a late-position maniac who has raised in front of you — then you have to reraise *if* you decide to play the hand. Either fold it or reraise it. Once a maniac has put in one raise, he's usually going to go for a second."

Of course, even a maniac can pick up a real hand. I wouldn't raise with this hand because any player can pick up a premium hand. I don't care if he knows how to play them or not, he can be dealt a good hand.

Let me give you an example: In a hold'em tournament, I had $2,500 in chips. I am never a person to put in all my chips with a hand like two queens, but I had played with this particular opponent for the entire tournament and noted that every time he had deuces through sixes in the first seat he brought it in for $250 — and then showed his hand on the end. So here he comes for $250 and I move in on him with two queens. This time he has two aces! It just goes to show you that anybody, no matter how low the quality of their play is, can pick up a hand. Over a long period of time, they're going to be dealt the same types of cards that you get, the good along with the bad.

In Omaha high-low tournaments, when you're playing four-handed or less (usually only at the final table) *then* you can play the big pairs. I won the Omaha high-low title at the World Series a few years ago with two nines over Chris Bjorin's two sixes, but very shorthanded like that is the only time that you can consider playing big pairs. In a full ring game with so many of the cards out of the deck, those high-pair hands are nothing, but four-handed there are only 16 cards off the deck, leaving 36 still in it. Some of the cards your opponents need may never come out, and there are a lot more cards left that can't hurt you, either. So even in Omaha high-low you can play those big pairs in four-handed tournament situations. But in a full ring game where the opposite is true — 36 cards are out with only 16 left in the deck — almost any card that comes off the deck is going to help somebody.

Trap Hands

There are some trap hands that you shouldn't play in Omaha high-low. Hands such as 3-4-5-6 are trap hands. If you get any action on the hand in a three or four-way pot, and the flop comes 7-2-K you might think that you have a pretty good low draw. But if somebody plays with you, he probably has an A-3 in his hand and you're in real bad shape. You want to stay away from these types of rundown hands — 7-6-5-4, 8-7-6-5, 6-5-4-3.

Even a 2-3-4-5 can be a trap: It looks just good enough to play if you're willing to draw to the 2-3 for low. A lot of people are going to play 2-3-4-5 because they're hoping to catch an ace on the flop and, in fact, you don't want to play an aceless 2-3 hand unless you also have the 4-5. However, if no ace comes on the flop you only have the third best low to draw to ... and then what do you do with the hand?

Of course, like everything else in life, there are exceptions to the rule here and there. For example, I was in the big blind in a tournament when we were at the $150-$300 level. I had been watching the players all day long, the hands they had been playing. A player raised from early position and there were three callers to me. I had J-10-9-7, a hand that I would just throw in the muck 99 times out of 100. But I thought, "None of these guys are playing these kinds of cards. They have all the low cards and all the superhigh cards, so those 16 cards are gone already. I'm gonna take a flop to this hand for

$300. If it comes with middle cards, I'm the one who has them." I wound up scooping the pot. The flop came 8-9-4, the turn was a queen, and they all called the action. "Let's put a king out there now," I said to myself, calling for my ideal card. Sure enough, there it came.

Now, why did I play this hand? First, I knew how the others guys played, the kinds of cards they came in with. Second, I couldn't be raised, so I decided to take a shot with the hand. This isn't something that I recommend doing, but if you want to get a hold of some chips in a tournament, you do some rare things once in a while.

Although I might have made the same play in a ring game, remember that in a cash game where people can go to their pockets they play a lot of strange hands, so it might not be too smart to play those kinds of cards. But in a tournament it's different. In tournaments the kinds of cards people play is pretty cut and dried. "This is why you have to be a little more flexible at times in tournaments," Tom adds. "You have an advantage when you have a pretty fair idea what cards they have and they do *not* have an idea about what you have. Then when you have cards that you're fairly certain are live, and it won't cost you much, you might play a hand that you wouldn't otherwise play."

It all depends on how the game is being played at your table at that time. Every player is different. Every table is different. In the postmortems of every tournament, you hear players say, "That was a hand he shouldn't have played," or "How could he have raised that those cards?" People have different styles of play, but I contend that there is a "right" style, too, and that is what we're getting at in this book.

Another Trap Hand

K-Q-J-6, three high cards with a dangler. Who the hell wants to play that kind of hand?! I've seen players call half a bet with hands like that in the small blind in an unraised pot, but why waste the money? The only time you should be playing this type of hand is when you're dealt it in the big blind in an unraised pot.

Suppose you're playing in a tournament at the $400-$800 level and you're in the small blind for $200. It costs you $200 to complete the bet, and you do. If you don't flop anything to your K-Q-J-6 or Q-J-10-5, that's $200 lost. But with that same $200 in your stack in a later position, you might get four-way action (including yourself) and that $200 becomes $800. At a later period you could win $600 or $800 with that $200 you lost. You have to think about these things all the time, because in tournament play you can't go to your pocket.

For example, say that you call a $500 bet in a no-limit hold'em tournament that you're not supposed to call. Later on, that $500 could've meant $1,000 to you because you could've gotten that $500 doubled up — the same $500 that you didn't have because you called a bet earlier with an inferior hand.

A Tip From the Top
Always think like a pilot and fly ahead of the plane. Plan your strategy in advance.

You should always be thinking like a pilot, flying ahead of the plane. Always think in advance about the consequences of your play. "If I make this call with $300 of my $1,000 in chips and lose the hand, I'll have $700 left. If I could double up my $1,000 I'd have $2,000, but if I double up $700 I'll only have $1,400." The idea is to get all the chips, so you need to be taking all of these factors into consideration every time you make a decision. Actually, you shouldn't even have to think about it — once you know these concepts they should become ingrained in your mind.

When you're studying whether to call (the "long" call), it shouldn't even have to be a "study" for you — your decision should come automatically, quickly. Of course, Dana says that I'm mostly talking about players like myself who are on "automatic pilot," as she calls it. That's true, but that's why we're putting these things in this book — so that you can learn how to do these things, and so that you can develop your own automatic pilot.

PLAYING ON THE FLOP

If you flop the nuts and you can't be counterfeited, you can let them come to you. If you don't have the stone nuts, you'll have to gamble a little bit. If the flop comes with two low cards and you have four low cards working toward the nuts, you'll be playing the hand and you'll be playing it strong.

Position really doesn't matter in a situation like that. The only thing that position does for you is provide you with more information in a situation where you're in an end position, or you're on fourth street, and they start checking to you. If you're there (that is, you've made your hand), you might be able to start maximizing your bets. But of all the games I've played, I think that Omaha high-low is the least positional game there is. This is a hand dominated game. Tom adds, "That's because so many people find an excuse to be in the pot that making a late-position raise, or even an early-position raise, doesn't have nearly the impact that it does in other games." That's true, plus Omaha high-low is a limit game.

A Tip from the Top
The more people in the pot with you
the less important your position.

The more people there are in the pot, the less important position becomes. For example, your position in limit hold'em is a strong consideration if you're playing heads-up. When your opponent checks to you in a heads-up hand, you might be able to represent something that will make him throw his hand away. But if there are three or four players still in the pot, chances are that you can't make all of them fold. How often can you make that many players throw away their hands?

Position works strictly in proportion to the number of players who are in the pot with you in almost any limit game. The more players in the pot the less important position is in limit games, and the more important is hand value. Because it's a limit game, and because most pots are played multiway, Omaha high-low is a hand-value game. In pot-limit Omaha, even with three or four players in the pot, position is so much stronger than it ever will be in any limit game.

Therefore, I suggest that you play your hand straightforward in Omaha high-low most of the time. A lot of people trap in this game when they have huge hands, but those big hands don't come out very often. In the everyday play of the game, simply bet your hand because position is never as important as it is in a pot-limit or no-limit game.

In poker, some great hands play themselves ... and some terrible hands play themselves. It is the "decision" hands where you win or lose the money.

Reading the Board

You have to be a good reader in Omaha high-low. There are so many times when you can tell by the action that you might get only a fourth of the pot or less with your ace-deuce, so it's not worth putting your money in. You know that you have a nut low, but you also know that there are a couple of other nut lows out there after the flop.

Suppose the flop comes with two spades. You can't make a flush but you have a good shot at the nut low (or you already have the nut low) and there's action that tells you that somebody has a set, somebody has the spade draw, and a couple of other players have an ace-deuce (along with you). A lot of times, you might as well just throw that hand away, especially if you don't have another low card to go with your ace-deuce. Why get involved with it when the best you probably can do is get a third of the low end?

When You Flop the Nut Straight

Suppose you're in the big blind in an unraised pot and you have middle cards. The flop comes out and you make the nut straight. How do you play it?

If there is no pair and there are three different suits on board, you might want to push the hand very strongly. If you flop a straight *draw* and the flop comes out with a pair *and* two to your middle straight draw, you'd better play it very softly, if at all. If there are three flush cards out there, you'd better forget it. And if it comes with two of a suit, you would play it a little slower (even though you have a made straight) until fourth street at least, because if the third suited card comes, someone usually has the flush. Remember that you can flop the nuts and lose it on the turn.

"If it's possible, it's probable" is the expression that Dana used in her book for low-limit Omaha high-low players. The whole idea is that if you're playing against one person, the probability of your hand holding up is a lot higher than it is if you're in a multiway pot. So, you determine your play by the number of players in the pot.

"Remember that with four cards working in the hands," Tom adds, "there will always be more flushes out there, more sets and more full houses. The nuts will almost always be there, especially in eight-or-better games." That's particularly true in low-limit games where so many pots are played multiway. And as we said earlier, when you play four high or semi-high straight cards, you always want to have two cards that can make a straight to the ace, so you at least need to have a J-10 in the hand.

Now let's look at another middle-straight hand. Suppose you are in the big blind in an unraised, multiway pot and you have this hand:

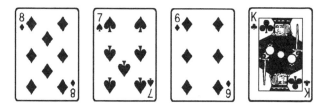

The flop comes:

You've flopped the nuts. You know the ace-deuces are probably out and they have made a wheel. How do you play the hand? With two of a suit out there, just check and call.

Now, what if you have A♣ K♦ 9♥ 8♣ in the same scenario and the flop comes 10♥ J♠ Q♥. Again you have the nut straight, this time with an all-high board. What do you do? Same thing — check and call. It's the same formula as the first hand ... your hand is only the nuts at the moment.

Going back to the seven-high straight you made in the first example above, who's going to make a higher straight than you? Nobody. In the second example where you made the ace-high straight on the flop, it's the same concept: Nobody can make a higher straight that yours. But when two of the same suit are on the board and there's any action on the flop, there's a chance that the flush draw is out or possibly a set so why not play this hand slow to start with? After fourth street when the third suited card hasn't shown up and there's only one card to come, then play it strong. It's the same theory as in pot-limit Omaha: You have to be very careful on the flop. (That's the only poker game where you throw away the nuts on the flop a lot of times.) You just have to use your head in these situations.

A Tournament Hand. This time, let's look at a hand that was played in a five-way, unraised pot in a $100 buy-in Omaha high-low tournament. The lady in the big blind held:

The flop came:

She checked the nut low from up front, and it was bet and called all the way around. She also flat called. The turn came with the 6♣. Again she checked and it was bet and called all the way around and again she also called. On the river came the J♣. This time she bet first and only one player called. She scooped the pot with the nut low and a pair of eights.

Her thought was that by betting first on the river, she was representing the backdoor flush and, of course, she had a lock on the nut low. Later, she asked my opinion of how she had played the hand.

I analyzed it this way: Why didn't she lead at this pot on the flop? Especially since she had a pair to go with the nut low? But since she decided to check on the flop, she certainly should have raised after it was bet and the action came back to her. In limit poker it is almost 90 percent "pure" that anyone who calls a bet on the flop will call a raise on the flop — you see this happen all the time. If you check with this hand, you do it for only one reason — to check-raise it and maximize your money in the pot. And from that point on, you have to bet first. If her nut low had been counterfeited on fourth street, she simply could've thrown it away.

"If she hadn't had a pair to go with the nut low," Tom adds, "it would have been correct for her to check and call, but the eight gave her an extra out." Right — what happens if another eight comes on fourth street? There's a pretty good chance that nobody would fill up since there was no significant action on the flop.

After she checked on the flop, she definitely should have bet out on the turn, especially when a random card (a jack) came. "By leading with the nut low on fourth street after checking it on the flop, you create confusion in your opponents' minds," Tom adds. "They don't know what that turn card has done for you, if anything." Plus, since the bets are double on fourth street, some people who might have called the single bet on the flop may not call the bet on fourth street, so you might be able to reduce the field of people drawing against you when you bet on fourth street.

"And you have played the hand in a rather unorthodox way," Tom says, "adding to their confusion and making them guess. When you put your opponents to the guess, they usually guess wrong." This is a good example of a situation where good players will always maximize their win. This player won at least four bets less than she should've won on the hand.

When the Flop Comes with Wheel Cards

Suppose the pot has been raised before the flop and you have called the raise with:

The action is now four-handed and the flop comes with:

Someone in an early position bets and you're next to act. Since your deuce was counterfeited on the flop, you now have a pair and an inside wheel draw. Do you call?

Of course not! Anytime you're certain that someone has already made a wheel, why would you call? You're only going for a split, to win half the pot at the best, *if* you catch a three. And if you catch, somebody probably will make a higher straight and you'll wind up with a fourth of the pot.

You'll see players in low-limit games making these types of calls all the time. Of course, you want to see this happening — you don't want to be the person doing it, you want to be the person with the wheel with them trying to make the hand.

Now suppose you have the same hand as in the first example and three wheel cards come on the flop with two cards in your suit:

You haven't made a wheel, but you have the nut-flush draw (or suppose you've made a set). Do you draw? If I'm certain that somebody has already made the wheel, I'm throwing the hand away. In Omaha high-low the idea is to scoop pots. Anytime you can scoop a pot, you're ahead of the game. So, if you have to call a raise cold and you think there's already a wheel out there when all you have is a draw, I can't see any percentage in playing further.

In this same four-way pot, suppose someone leads at the flop, the next player just flat calls, and now it's up to you. Do you call? Theoretically, no. If the player who flat-called cannot be counterfeited, he probably wouldn't raise on the flop, he'd wait to raise on fourth street when the bets are double. "In this scenario, I might call the single bet," Tom says. "I have the nut-flush draw and it's only going to cost me one single bet with at least two and possibly three other people in the pot, although I'm taking the risk that the player behind me might raise."

Now here's where position can become important in Omaha high-low: If you're the last to act, you can call the bet because you're thinking, "Since the action is in front of me, if the wheel is out I'll know it on fourth street." If someone has the wheel, he will certainly raise it on fourth street when the bets double, and you're sitting behind him. But if you're in early position, it's different. So long as you're sitting behind the other players, you have the advantage of position and can determine what to do on fourth street from the action in front of you. The final word is that if it isn't raised, there's nothing wrong with making a call — but if you believe the wheel is out, just throw the hand away.

A Tip From the Top
Always follow your instincts.
When you're in doubt, dump it.

Always go with your instincts, with what you've learned from playing over the years. A good rule of thumb in Omaha high-low is this: Any time you're in doubt about a hand, get rid of it. When you're in doubt, dump it.

A lot of players will catch such a monster flop that they don't want to lose anybody. Maybe it comes with two of a suit and two wheel cards, and they have the complete wrap wheel draw with the nut-flush draw. Naturally, they don't want to lose anybody early. Even if they make it on fourth street, they won't raise — they'll wait until fifth street because they want to get at least one bet out of you on the end. And when the limits go up in a tournament, that isn't a bad play at all because they can win a lot of money on the end that way.

Playing a High Hand

If you have the high hand and you know that you're up against one or more low hands, you're going to be very, very aggressive with it. Any time you have the high nuts (except when you flop a straight with two suited cards on board, as we discussed earlier), you should be rammin' and jammin' just hoping a couple of players are drawing for low.

"But suppose you've had the high hand all along with a couple of opponents drawing at the low," Tom adds. "On the river comes a third low card and somebody fires a bet in front of you. You know that you have half of the pot in your pocket, but there's a player left to act behind you. In this scenario, a flat call might be better than a raise because you want to entice the third player to overcall, especially if you think he also has a low." However, if you're the last to act when there's been a bet and a call in front of you, you definitely should raise in order to maximize your win.

"You don't care if there's a reraise and the third guy folds," Tom says, "because you're still going to win the same amount of money."

Let me put it this way — if you're in a tournament and it's your mother who's sitting to your left ... and she's the one who led at it and got two callers ... and you're in last position, you raise!

"Mom," Tom says that he would tell her, "you've just gotta learn how to play better!"

Playing a Drawing Hand in a Side Game

When you have a strong draw in Omaha high-low, and you're in a front position, how far do you take it? I'd bet it on the flop but I'm not saying that I would bet it on fourth street where it's a double bet. I like to lead on the flop with it ... that's fine ... and if you're playing heads-up, there's nothing wrong with leading at it again on fourth street. But if you're in a multiway pot, you shut down on fourth.

You see, when you're against only one other guy, by betting on fourth street you're setting up a bet on fifth street if you think he's going low. But against two or three other players, betting on fourth street doesn't set anything up for you. One of your opponents might be playing high and the other one might be playing low, so you're in a different situation. I'm not saying that you don't call, just that you don't lead at the pot. Actually, you're hoping to get a free card.

But you see so many people continue to push their draws in the lower-limit games, $4-$8 up to $10-$20. If you want to see how Omaha high-low *should* be played, watch Paul and Jack from Phoenix. They're never overly aggressive unless they have a very strong hand on the flop. They make all their moves *later* in the play, always at the double-bet level. Remember that when you raise at one of the two-bet levels, it's worth a lot more to you. And usually, if a guy has a lot of money invested in the pot he'll call that extra bet.

Key Concept. "It is only sophisticated players with a lot of discipline who will delay their action until fourth or fifth street," Tom notes. "Players with average skills who just like betting the nuts all the time don't realize that they sometimes can make more money by delaying their action." But that's part of adjusting to the game, too.

If you're in a game where everybody's calling everything all the way through, why not lead with your hand? You don't have to wait until fourth or fifth streets because you're going to get them to play anyway. But when you're in there against some decent players, a lot of times you'll delay your action so you can get as much as possible out of the pot. The caliber of your opposition always affects your strategy.

Saving Bets

In the limit hold'em games, you'll see somebody lead at the pot with an ace when it gets checked to him. If he gets raised, he automatically calls. Ninety-nine out of a hundred players will call that first raise. He might just have an ace and you might have a set, but he's going to try to catch an ace for himself when there's a low flop. Sometimes it works for him, but I'll bet that if he charted his play over a year's time, he'd find that he's a losing player.

Remember that in *all* limit games, unless you've had a rush of cards, the bets you save will be what you win at the end of the day. While X, Y, and Z have been making those long calls, you haven't — and that's going to be your profit margin at the end of the day. The cards will break even over a long period of time.

"Do you mean that even if you have the nut flush draw and the nut-low draw on the flop," Dana asks, "if you're in early position and you don't make it on the turn, you're going to check?" You're damn right I am — in limit games. And in no-limit games, the worst play you can make is to be in last position and bet a draw with one card to come, when you could've seen it for nothing. You've wasted a bet, plus you've wasted your chance to win the hand. Hopefully, your opponent is drawing at the same flush that you are but he's drawing at a lower one — and you both make it. The same concept

58

is true of Omaha high-low. On fourth street with one card to come, take your free draw if you're around back and nobody has bet. Why waste the bet?

"If you have a strong drawing hand on the flop and it's checked to you," Tom adds, "I'd certainly go ahead and bet it. A lot of times, you'll get the free card anyway because you have bet on the flop. But if you had checked on the flop, your opponents may feel more free to bet into you on the turn, forcing you to call the double-bet to see the river card. So it's actually cheaper for you to make the one-unit bet on the flop."

Getting a Free Card

Here's a situation where position comes into play. Say that you're around back and have a drawing hand on the flop and someone bets into you. In this situation, you raise it. Almost invariably, that raise will give you the free card on fourth street. If they called your bet on the flop, they'll think that you're the one with the strong hand going, so they'll check to you on fourth street. If you don't make your hand on fourth, you check along.

This is a limit hold'em play, but it works in any limit game when you want to get a free card. (I say "free" card, but actually it's a "half-a-bet" card because you've raised on the flop.) "The beauty of it is that if you make the hand," Tom adds, "since they're not sure you were on a draw, they very well may call you on the end."

Even if they make the hand on fourth street, some players will check it to get the call on the end. "That's an ultra-sophisticated play and it works well against either very bad players or very good players," Tom observes, "because it creates confusion." Yes, but I'll bet you that I could name more than 100 players who play it the same way *every* time. You *know* that if they checked on fourth street when the flush card came and then bet on fifth street, they made the flush and checked it on fourth. And so, you can get away from them because you know they play exactly the same way every time. That's why you have to change your play around a little bit.

Playing a Drawing Hand in a Tournament

Dana tells about a hand she played in a $200 buy-in Omaha high-low tournament: "I had an A-2-5-7 in a heads-up pot and a 3-4-10 flopped with no suits. My opponent checked and I bet. On the turn I didn't make my draw. He checked and I bet it again, thinking that since he was a strong player he wouldn't call me if he didn't have a hand. But he called. On the river the board paired and I had nothing. He bet first and I released the hand."

That's correct, you had no choice. But what would you have done if he had checked at the river? What if, just like you, he had just been drawing for the low? In a multiway pot you wouldn't bet it, but heads-up, why not? This is where the iron balls come in! In a multiway pot, you wouldn't bet it on the end *and* you wouldn't have bet on fourth street either.

Key Concept. Remember that a weak player usually won't call you if he doesn't have anything. There's a better chance of a strong player calling you than there is of a weak player calling you *on the end*. If the weak player knows he has nothing, he'll say, "Well, I can't beat anything." But the strong player might have an A-K, the top two cards that could possibly be out, no pair or anything, and call you. We've all done it.

I'll give you an example: In a one-table hold'em satellite I played, the board came 2♦ 2♥ 3♣. I was in the big blind with J♦ 6♠. The player right in front of me bet his hand and I called him. The turn came nothing. He bet and I called again.

On the end, he bet again and I called him. I took the pot with a jack-high.

Then a player says out loud, "I want to learn how to make that play!" And Jim Ward leans over to me and says, "The funny thing is, they think it's luck when you do that."

Ward recognized the play. I knew the other player and thought he was out of line, but I never raised at any time — I believed my jack-high was best and I wanted him to keep coming. "T. J. really put a dead read on the guy," Tom observed. "All he could have had to bet with was a 4-5 for a straight draw or something like that. It was just another situation where knowing your opponents is so important."

T. J. Cloutier and his wife Joy at the 1997 Queens Poker Classic

PLAYING THE TURN

Suppose you are in a front position in a multiway pot and you have:

The flop comes 3-5-K. You bet and two people call. The turn comes with a deuce:

Your low draw is counterfeited and there are three wheel cards on the board. What do you do?

Tom answers, "If I were against only one opponent who I think is semi-weak, I might consider betting to see his reaction. But with players left to act behind me in a multiway pot, and with three wheel cards on the board, I would check."

The main consideration is that you don't want to stand a raise with this hand, so you check the turn. If someone bets behind you, you fold the hand. After all, what do you have? Bottom two pair and an inside wheel draw against someone who may already have the wheel and maybe another player who thinks he can draw out with the top two pair.

Bluffing

"When your low draw gets counterfeited, couldn't you just go ahead and bet again on fourth street to represent the wheel, especially since you had bet first on the flop?" Let me tell you something about bluffing in limit Omaha high-low — it's ridiculous! I don't mean that you can *never* bluff: There *are* certain situations where you can run a bluff, but this isn't one of them.

But suppose you know that your opponent has a low draw because of the way he has played the hand. A set comes on the board at the end, and there is no low possibility. (When a set comes on the board, the best hand is the fourth card of that rank or the highest pair held in any player's hand.) You might bluff at this pot against *one* person. You've been trailing in the hand and he's been leading, so you might just win this hand with a bet on the end because you pretty well know that he doesn't have any pairs. This is one bluff you can make in Omaha high-low, but there are very few others.

"Here's another example of a bluff, one that I made in a $20-$40 game," Tom relates. "I was in an unraised pot in late position with a rundown hand that I normally wouldn't play, 5-6-7-9 suited. The flop came 8-4-Q. It was bet and called in two places, and I called with the inside straight draw. The turn card paired the four. The original bettor checked, everybody else checked, and I checked. On the river came a jack, making the board 8-4-Q-4-J with the possibility of a straight. Everybody had missed the low. When they all checked to me, I bet. One by one, they folded. This type of positional play sometimes works when you're certain that no one has made a hand either way."

There was only one downside to this play. What if someone had flopped two pair, made the full house on the turn, and checked twice with the intent of check-raising anybody who bet? "My opponents were playing quite straightforwardly," answers Tom, "so I didn't think that was the case, although the double check is a play that a sophisticated player might make in this situation. And too, there is one breed of very sophisticated player who might figure out that I was trying to steal the pot and would check raise me with nothing! Thankfully, I had read my opponents correctly and no one figured out my play."

Less Than the Nuts. "Are there times when you call with less than the nuts?" Dana asks. "For example, do you call with an A-3 when the board comes with three low cards?" If you have an A-10-3-4-or-5 with the ace suited, how could you not play your low draw? The A-2 isn't always out, you know.

"This is a case where the preflop action would determine my strategy," Tom explains. "If nobody has raised and I flop the second-nut low with my A-3, I would bet it in late position if it is checked to me. If I'm in an early position, I probably would check it if there had been any preflop raises. If everyone checked on the flop, I would lead with it on fourth street. I also would bet it at the river most of the time."

The Theory and the Reality

"In his book on split games, Ray Zee mentions that there is more difference in the way that low-limit and high-limit Omaha high-low games are played than in any other form of poker," Dana mentions. "Would you agree that in the low-limit games, you usually need to have the nuts to be in the pot whereas in the higher limit games you don't?"

Yes, I agree with that because in the higher-limit games there usually are fewer people involved in the pot than there are in lower-limit games, strictly because of the money. Remember, the more people in the pot, the more likely it is that the nuts is out. In low-limit games, players are peddling the nuts a lot more often than they do in higher-limit games. The theory of *how* to play is still the same for all limits, but the *actual* play is different.

The theory is that you play X-hand whether you're playing $1-$3 or $3,000-$6,000. But when it comes to the actual play of the game, you have to adjust to the size of the game and how your opponents are playing it. You might take a few more chances with your starting hands and on the flop in lower-limit games because it won't cost you much when you have a shot at the nuts, whereas in a higher-limit game it can cost you a bundle. With the theory that we're putting down in this book, you'll have a better chance of winning at any limit than you do by simply playing a little looser.

"So, the theory is that in lower limits you can play looser before the flop but you should play tighter after the flop," Dana summarized, "whereas in higher-limit games you play tighter before the flop and a little looser after the flop?"

Yes, I think that's what I just said, but they both *should* be played the same. If you have $100 to gamble and you're playing $1-$3, what's the difference in that and having $10,000 to gamble and playing a lot higher? Because you have a limited amount to gamble with, the play should be the same in both situations. The biggest difference is that you're up against a lot of maniacs in low-limit games, which changes the flow of everything. And it changes how the cards are boxed.

It doesn't matter how many times the cards are shuffled, they get boxed so that certain cards come out more often than other cards. In low-limit games, people who are playing a bunch of strange hands sometimes hit a lot of them because of this "boxing" effect. In theory you should play the same no matter what the limits, but in actuality I don't know anybody who doesn't play a little looser in the smaller games. If a high-limit player who can't find anything else to do sits down in a little low-limit game, his game might go to pot playing in that game whereas he's a great player when he plays high. Like Stuey Ungar used to say, "I've got no chance playing $5-$10 limit hold'em. No chance whatsoever."

Fancy Moves

Are any fancy moves possible at the lower limit games? Sometimes, but not too often. Let me tell you about a pretty good move that came down in a game. I missed my low and ended up with two pair, top and third, on the end. I knew that somebody had made a low. The man on my right bet, I called because I thought I had the high hand, and then the obvious low hand raised the pot, opening it up. The man on my right, who had both the nut low and the same two pair that I held, reraised to knock me out of the pot. He accomplished his mission. I give the guy an A+ for the play. He didn't have the nut high, but he figured that the reraise would knock me out if I also didn't have the nuts. So, instead of winning half of the pot (one quarter for low and one quarter for high), he won three-fourths of it.

"In the low-limit games, there are more players per pot but they're more passive, they limp in more often," Tom mentions, "whereas in the higher-limit games there is more raising, more aggression. They thin out the pot more often before the flop with their raises. In the lower-limit games, the raise is used for two reasons: to build the pot and to limit the field, but in the higher-limit games the raise is mostly used to thin the field."

Getting Trapped with the Second-Nut Low

There's a trap in Omaha high-low that a lot of people fall into on the flop or turn. Suppose there is a 3-4-5 on the board and someone has an A-6 in his hand. Some players just won't cut themselves loose from the hand. There may be all sorts of action on fourth street, but they play the hand anyway even though they have no outs. The wheel's out there and if the board's suited, somebody else probably has a flush. This happens all the time.

Just remember that if you're in a multiway pot with an A-6 in this situation, you'd better dump the hand. If it's possible, it's probable is the way Dana said it in her book on low-limit Omaha high-low. Why do people do this? Sometimes it happens after the first guy bets and you call. Then the action takes place *behind* you and the average player says, "Well, I called the first bet so I might as well call the next one." Then you're hooked into the pot.

PLAYING AT THE RIVER

"You could have the biggest draw in the world, the best high wraparound, the nut flush draw along with a wheel draw, and still wind up with nothing in Omaha high-low," Tom whines. "Sometimes I think this is the biggest drawout game in the world!" There may be a grain of truth in what Tom says, but that's one of the things that entices so many people into playing Omaha high-low. And that's also why it's so important to have an extra out, a second hand that you can draw to.

A Tip From the Top
Always try to have an extra out.

What happens when you've had the nut low all along and get counterfeited at the river so that you now have the second-nut low? How you play it is determined by the action.

"If you're first to bet you're forced to check and then judge your best move by the action after you" Tom explains . "But suppose you've been counterfeited for the nut low and all hell breaks loose in front of you ... for example, there's a bet and a raise before it gets to you, or there is a bet and a couple of callers. With substantial action in front of you, you have to reevaluate whether your hand is worth a play. If there's a bet and a raise — especially if the raise comes from someone that you suspect is on a low hand, not a high hand — your hand should automatically become history.

"However, say that a player who you think is on a high hand leads at the pot and only one or two others call but they don't raise. In this case, your hand may be worth an overcall, mainly because one of the callers may have a weaker low, or at the least, a hand that ties yours. Therefore, it's worth a bet even if you get only a quarter of the pot since the pot is a substantial size.

"What you can't do is to call a bet and a raise, or put yourself in danger of being raised after you have acted. For example, suppose someone leads into the pot at the river and you are next to act with two or three people yet to act behind you. You have to pass because you're in danger of getting raised and/or reraised. You can't take the chance of throwing in a bet because you can't handle a raise — unless you have a dead read that no one is likely to raise you. All you can do in this situation is make a crying call for one single bet and even then, if a rock still to act looks like he's going to make a long call, you'd better reevaluate. Sometimes the rocks won't put in a raise with the nut low or second nut low because they're afraid of getting quartered, so you have to use judgment.

"As a general rule to go by, when I have the second-nut low at the river and the pot is substantial, I will call if I think there's a reasonable chance that I might get at least a quarter of the pot and it's only going to cost me one more bet."

Determining the Best High Hand

"If somebody bets and two or three players just call in front of you at the river," Dana says, "it sometimes is difficult to determine whether the callers have a low hand or a high hand. Let's assume that the first bettor has a high hand. If no flushes or straights are possible, it may be difficult for a high hand to know for sure whether he has the best high and so, he may call with a hand that he thinks might take the high half of the pot. If you have a low hand but have been counterfeited, you may still have the best low or be tied for it even when someone bets and two players call in front of you."

Tom adds: "In fact, the best high is more difficult to determine than the best low. You *always* know where you are on the low — you know what the best possible low hand is — but you don't always know whether your high hand is the best. Suppose the board reads A-6-J-4-9. The best low is 2-3 and the best possible high is trip aces. But the best high hand being played by an opponent could be trip jacks, or top two pair, or even bottom set.

"It's easy to read the nut low but it isn't always clear what the high is. Sometimes the best high is an overpair or a weak two-pair or a low set, maybe even a one-pair hand. Sometimes, too, a high hand might lead at the pot and an even better high hand will only smooth call because he wants all of the lows in there so he can get a half of their money. And the nut lows often use that same strategy to win a bigger half of the pot."

Betting the Nut Low

You cannot bet the low on the end if that's all you have. You don't even have to *know* that there's another low hand out there, or that there's a probability of its being out there — you can *sense* it. You can't bet it *unless* you're playing against one other person who you think might be drawing for high and you think that you might be able to scoop the pot from him. For example, maybe you have a pair along with the low — or maybe you don't even have a pair, but you think you can get by with representing one.

"Some low-limit players insist on betting the nut low with nothing else," Tom adds, "when it's obvious to any decent player that there's another nut low out." You see that happen in tournaments all the time. All of the good players will simply check. A player told me about a hand he played in an Omaha high-low tournament. He flopped the nut low up front in a multiway pot and check-called the hand all the way. On the river the button raised, he called, and so did a third player. The button turned over the nut low and the two of them were quartered by the high hand. "Man, how could you have kept checking that nut low?" the button asked him.

I gave him a standard answer: "Buddy, when you learn how to play this game, come back and ask me that question again." Usually I let everything go by, but every now and then I'll get my dander up and put people in their place.

The main thing that we need to stress is this: If you've been betting the low hand in a pot where there's been three-way action all the way — and you know there's one high hand — you cannot bet your low hand on the end because you're probably getting quartered. When you only have a one-way hand, you're making more money for the other guy than you are for yourself!

A Move on the River in Tournament Play

Dana tells this story: "In a $300 buy-in Omaha high-low tournament with three tables left when the limits were quite high, I was in the big blind in an unraised pot and there were two other players in the hand. I didn't know the player in the middle but I knew the guy in third position to be a high-limit, aggressive cash game player. The flop came with A♠ Q♦ 5♣, no suits. I checked, the middle man bet, and the third player and I both called. On the turn came the 9♣, giving me an inside-straight draw, a low draw, and a weak four-flush. Again, it was check, bet, call, call. The river card was the Q♣. I checked, the second player bet, and the third player raised. I thought about calling, but with no low and only a little flush against what was probably a full house, I folded. The player in the middle called with an A-10. The third played showed an A-K. Neither had a flush or full-house, not even a set!"

The third man simply made a move at the pot, that's all. Your play was right. "Yes, but I lost the pot! I made the right play but got the wrong result." Let me tell you something important here: If you cannot lay down a winner in poker, you cannot win. Otherwise, you're a calling station and you're a goner. Remember that.

Knowing Your Opponents

Yesterday I lost money in a $40-$80 game, but I learned something about a player that I hadn't played with before. He always *always* check-raised on the flop if he had a hand. Not once did he ever lead. What does this tell me? I'm never going to bet any marginal hands on the flop when this man is in the pot. If I bet, I'm going to have the goods when he's in the pot with me. In the long run, that knowledge will save me a lot of money. In any game you play, no matter what the limits, you have to learn your opponents and learn them well.

Suppose the flop comes K-Q-4 and you have a king and queen in your hand. You bet and get called in a couple of spots. On fifth street comes a jack. You check and your opponent bets. If you've been watching the game and you know how he plays, you might say to yourself, "I know he didn't make a straight. I've got this man tied in this hand," and you make the call. But if you haven't been watching how he plays, you might automatically give him credit for the straight and lay down your hand.

There are situations where you have to call if you know the type of player who's making the bet — when *you* know that he's a good enough player to make the bet with kings and queens to represent the straight when there's a K-Q-J on the board — and *he* knows that you're a good enough player to throw the hand away. ♣

Chapter 3

POT-LIMIT OMAHA

by T. J. Cloutier
Commentary by Tom McEvoy

Pot-limit Omaha is the biggest money game played today. With equal blinds, it is about three or four times the size of pot-limit hold'em and when it is played, it usually is the biggest poker game in the casino. A few Southern California cardrooms are now spreading it. The blinds in their pot-limit hold'em games are $10-$20 and the blinds in the pot-limit Omaha games are $5-$10. Actually, the blinds should be something like $15-$30 or even $20-$40 in the hold'em games and $5-$10 in the Omaha games to get a true comparison between the size of the two games.

This is the most treacherous poker game of all, but it also is the best game for making a big score. If you can get lucky and catch some cards and flops — and play right — you can make more money in pot-limit Omaha than you can in any other game.

Pot-limit Omaha is the only poker game in which you might throw away the nuts on the flop and be correct in doing so. It's also a game in which, if you flop top set and there are two of a suit and two connectors showing on the board, you could be in jeopardy. But it's a hand that you have to play — and a lot of times, you get killed with it.

The Betting Structure. In many pot-limit side games you have to come in for twice the big blind as your opening bet. If the big blind is $100 in a side game you have to bring it in for $200, which is not a raise, just the opening bet. This is done so that the blinds don't get a freeroll in side games. They have to put more money in the pot to see the flop. But in tournaments, that isn't true. In tournaments you can "gypsy" in — you can come in for the same price as the big blind. "However, most cardrooms are allowing players to gypsy in in side games, too, in order to emulate the tournament structure," Tom adds.

Compared to pot-limit Omaha, Omaha high-low is a relatively small game. But because it's played limit, the split game has become very popular. High Omaha has such fluctuations that it burns up a lot of money, and that's one reason why a lot of low-limit players have switched to Omaha high-low. Right now, the biggest pot-limit Omaha game in the nation is at the Horseshoe in Tunica, Mississippi, on the weekends. They play $25-$50 blinds and most of the players straddle it with $100. It doesn't sound that big because of its ante structure but there's always a lot of money on the table.

When they straddle it with $100, you can bring it in for $400, four times the big blind. If one guy calls $400 and another guy calls $400, now the next guy can call $400 and raise $1,600. If all four of them call for $1,600 there's $6,400 in the pot and the next bet can be $6,400 on the flop. If there is some play on the flop and it gets called, then you have three times that amount, which is $19,200 in the pot on the flop. You can see how it can tear you apart moneywise. It escalates at a high scale, but it's fun to play and if you really want to gamble, you'll find people gambling with some very strange hands. This is one reason why you'll always see more multiway action in pot-limit Omaha games than in pot-limit hold'em games.

Players who love pot-limit Omaha will travel long distances for a tournament just because there are one or maybe two events to play. They have very little interest in playing the other tournaments, but they know that all the big pot-limit players will be there and they probably will get a few side games going. At all the major tournaments, there's always a lot of pot-limit side action going.

Pot-limit Omaha is the best game to make money but it's also the toughest game. During the major tournaments, we used to have four or five $5-$10-$25 no-limit hold'em games and three $25-$25-$50 no-limit hold'em games until pot-limit Omaha came in — now we usually have only one pot-limit hold'em game and no no-limit hold'em games. For that reason, I'm sorry that pot-limit Omaha became so popular with the money players. When they want to play for big money these days they play pot-limit Omaha, not no-limit hold'em, which is my favorite game.

Last year at the World Series, we played a pot-limit Omaha game with $100-$200 blinds with an $8,000 buy-in, and we played a $200-$400 game with a $20,000 buy-in. And the games were full all the time! I played and so did Sammy Farquhar, Lindy Chambers, Howard Greenspan, Roger Moore ... there was a big field of players ... Tony Dee, Eskimo Clark, Phil Hellmuth. Of course, when they play that high it's going to bust a lot of people. (And when they play really high, even higher than these two games, Lyle Berman is the best player, in my opinion.) I never played more than two hours at a time for four nights in a row and I won $57,000 in that game. I suppose I could've won $157,000 in that length of time ... or I could've lost that much.

Actually, I wouldn't have lost that much. A lot of the high-stakes players these days will take chances and lose more money than they stand to win. As far as I'm concerned, that's the biggest fault of a lot of players. It's called eating like a bird and crapping like an elephant. When you win a little bit, you quit. When you lose, you go for almost your whole bankroll. It's easy to do in pot-limit Omaha.

That's why you have to have discipline when you play this game. Unless it's your last bit of money, you shouldn't lose your entire bankroll in any one poker game, Omaha, hold'em, no matter what it is. The idea is to quit and play another day, give yourself a chance. But there are players who do it time and time again.

A Tip from the Top
You must have discipline in pot-limit Omaha.
You shouldn't lose your whole bankroll
in one session.

I know a player from Texas who is so good at pot-limit Omaha, he will play for six months at a time and win every session. But he's the type of player who, if he gets on a losing streak in the game, if he has $100,000 it'll all go in that one game. Then he'll fly back home, get refinanced, and come back again. To me, this just does not make sense. People think that because they've gotten loser and have escaped the trap a couple of times and gotten their money back, they can do it every time.

Very seldom do you get a live one, a person who can't play at all, playing in these big games but it does happen sometimes. I know a player who, when he first came on the scene a few years ago and played high, would reraise with any four suited cards. It didn't matter what size they were or if they were connected. If the pot has been raised and three or four players were in it, he would reraise it. Everybody knew he was going to do this. He was just asking to go broke ... and they accommodated him. Of course, he put a lot of pressure on the game and he won a lot of pots because he got some funny flops and stuff. But in the long run, he had to lose.

Again, you have to use some discipline when you're playing cards, and he didn't have any. This year at the Series, though, he played completely different. He tried to play solid and things worked out better for him; he at least broke even. He had made some big scores at blackjack and brought that money over to the game with him. "It's usually just the opposite," Tom observed. "People make big scores at poker and take them to the blackjack tables and blow it off."

Implied Odds

"Implied odds are the future bets that you can expect to win if you get the right flop to your hand, and your opponent(s) do not read you correctly and give you too much action," Tom explains. "A lot of pot-limit Omaha hands have much higher implied odds than in limit Omaha.

"Sometimes you can win gigantic pots in pot-limit games with cards that aren't great starting hands *if* you play them in exactly the right situations against the right people — they can be enormous money makers. In this sense, pot-limit Omaha is somewhat like no-limit hold'em in that if you have a small pair and can get in cheap with it, or if it just costs a tiny little raise that won't cost you too much, you have enormous implied odds with a little hand that you're not going to play further unless you catch a favorable flop.

"For example, suppose you have 9-8-7-6 or 8-7-6-5 and you know that your opponent has big stuff. You can call a modest bet. You can play this type of hand before the flop for a small raise, too. Remember that the pots start out small in pot-limit and don't get bigger until a couple of rounds of betting are already in the pot.

"To summarize, when there's either a single minimum bet or a modest raise, you can play four connecting cards that you know aren't the best hand at the moment. In fact, you're sure that your opponent, who is a pretty solid player, has a big pair, but you also know that you have cards that are totally unrelated to his hand. It isn't going to cost you an arm and leg to see the flop so you can call the bet or modest raise. Your opponent doesn't know for sure where you're at, but you know where he's at. You have big implied odds in this hand."

Playing Sets

A set has less value in pot-limit Omaha than in any other poker game. The big thing about pot-limit Omaha is that it's a rarity when there are no straights and no flushes possible on the board when five cards are out. You can flop a set, even top set, and be a big dog if you get played with.

I'll never forget one time when Mansour Matloubi and I were in a game together. I raised with aces and the flop came A♥ Q♣ 4♥. Mansour had K♥ J♥ 10♦ 9♠. If I don't pair the board, I'm a big dog in this hand although I have the best hand at the moment. I bet, he raised and we got all the money in on the flop. "You can't win," Mansour says to me. "You have three aces and you can't win." Well, I knew that I could win: He could rag off or the board could pair. But it didn't — the first card off made the straight for him and the river card made the flush.

Tom tells about a similar experience he once had against Bob Ciaffone: "I flopped top set with pocket jacks with no straight or flush possible for me. Although two suited cards and a connecting card came on the flop, I had the nuts at that moment. He bets, I raise, and he puts me in. 'Gee, I wish I had more money,' I mumbled. And Ciaffone says, 'Hey, Tom, if you like your hand that much, I'll let you go into your pocket for another $500.' I thought about it for a moment and said OK. Of course I lost. He had a gigantic wraparound straight draw plus a flush draw, and he knew exactly what I had, so he cheerfully allowed me to put more money into the pot."

Bottom Set. Unless you're playing just one man, you'd better play very, very carefully with bottom set, even on a broken board. Say the flop comes J-7-3 and you have a pair of threes in the hole. Somebody starts firing at you. What are you going to do with this hand? What are you going to give him, 10-9-8?!

In limit high Omaha, if someone leads into you on the flop and you raise to build the pot, sometimes your opponent will fold and sometimes he will call. But suppose he reraises. Does the reraise mean that he has you beat? That's where your poker skills come in. However, whether or not he actually has you beat, you still play it ... but that's *limit* Omaha.

In pot-limit if you raise him to build a pot, he can put a monster reraise on you. Then what do you do? What I'm saying is that you can play the hand on the flop but you don't have to raise with it. If you raise and get reraised, your trip threes are probably a piece of cheese, so be very careful when you flop bottom set.

Knowing Your Opponents

When you're playing in a pot-limit Omaha game or tournament where you don't know the players, you have to find out which players will raise before the flop with which kinds of hands. A big percentage of players will raise with aces with connectors or aces double suited, and there are players who will raise with connecting cards like A-K-Q-J all the way down to 6-5-4-3. You have to know who will raise with what before the flop.

"Having a backdoor draw helps sometimes, too," Tom adds. "For example, when I'm playing against a guy who I know has aces, and I have a pair or a couple of three-flushes or a middle buster (an inside straight draw) with second pair, I might go after the guy. But you have to have a dead read on him. This is where knowledge of your opponents, which we harped on in our first book, comes into play."

Harped on? Well, let's harp on it some more! Here's something else you should find out about your opponents: Who will lead with a draw and who won't? Some players never make any moves, they just play the percentages. They're looking to show down the best hand every time. They wait forever to get a big hand to play, and hope they get a flop to their hands when they play them.

The Size of Your Bets

How do you judge the size of your bets in pot-limit Omaha? It's almost "pure" that you always raise the size of the pot if you have a hand. The concept of building the pot that is true of pot-limit hold'em does not apply to pot-limit Omaha because Omaha pots get built automatically.

Generally speaking, no one comes in for a raise that is less than the size of the pot. You don't see $500 in the pot and bet $100 at it. "In other words, you don't make a small bet to try to pick up a big pot. But you do occasionally see bad players try that," Tom adds. "Their underbet is a tip-off: They're just tipping you off that they have a big hand and want to get called. An inexperienced player, or a weak player who's afraid he won't get paid off on a hand, might bet $100. But if you keep your bets standard rather than betting in some sort of pattern, your opponents won't know where you're at by comparing the size of your bet relative to the strength of your hand." Remember, too, that in pot-limit you can say "I bet the pot." Then the dealer counts it down for you.

A Tip from the Top
The pot will always get big enough in pot-limit.

Remember this about pot-limit Omaha: The pot's going to get big enough. You don't have to build it before the flop — it *will* get big enough. This game can chew up your money so fast, it'll make your head spin. You play, you win four or five little pots of $500 to $1,000 each, you have $4,000 in front of you — that entire $4,000 could be in the pot before the flop in the next big hand!

Raising in Tournaments

Lyle Berman once told me that in a tournament, no hand is big enough to raise with before the flop because you're committing too much money for tournament play. If you raise with your aces before the flop you're committing a lot of money to it that you don't necessarily have to until you see the flop.

If you find a situation in which someone raises and there are a couple of callers, then you can *reraise*, but you don't put in the initial raise yourself. You see, when there's a raiser and a couple of callers, then it's worth it to reraise with your aces and connectors or suits because the pot is big enough so that you can raise enough money to shut somebody out, to narrow it down to you and one other person. This is where you can raise with your aces.

"In tournament play there are always exceptions to this strategy," Tom inserts. "If I am short-stacked, I am more likely to raise the maximum before the flop with aces, even if I am the first one in. Also, if I have a large stack against players with short or medium stacks, I will put the heat on them with aces, especially if I think that they are in their survival mode. These are the main exceptions about raising early with aces in tournament play."

Insurance in Pot-Limit Omaha

Insurance is laid either on the flop or on fourth street. Usually, the time when insurance comes up is when two guys are heads-up with a lot of money in the pot and one of them is all-in. In an insurance deal, the best hand will take odds against your drawing out on him. Then you figure out the number of outs the worst hand has.

You never get the true price on insurance. Let's say that you have the nut flush draw and your opponent has a set with two cards to come. You have 18 outs to make the flush, unless he has two lower flush cards and in that case, you're down to seven times two for 14 outs. Twenty-eight outs is an even hand. On that basis, he is a 2-to-1 favorite with two cards to come. And with one card to come, you have seven outs versus 28, and he is a 4-to-1 favorite.

The player who asks for insurance is the one who is in the lead with the best hand. If you are in the lead, you have to be willing to give up some of the price. If you're a 2-to-1 favorite, you probably can get 8-to-5 at the best. If you're a 4-to-1 favorite, you might get 3-to-1 insurance at the tops. If there is $5,000 in the pot, the underdog might say, "You take $3,000, I'll take $1,000 and we'll play for the other $1,000." This is one type of insurance.

Another type of insurance occurs when a player who isn't in the hand wants to lay you insurance. He might say, "I'll lay you 8-to-5, what do you want it for? I'll lay you $8,000 to $5,000." If you win the pot, you have to give him $5,000. If you lose it, he gives you $8,000. Or if the insurance proposition is 2-to-1, you have to give him $5,000 if you win but if you lose, he has to give you $10,000.

Another form of insurance that is very popular these days involves running the cards twice. You might do it on fourth street or you might do it on fifth street only. Suppose all the money's in and now you want to do insurance. You have the draw and your opponent has the hand. Then somebody says, "OK, we'll run 'em twice."

When you run them twice, you're playing for half the pot each time. The dealer burns and turns, burns and turns, and then you figure out who won the first deal. If the board rags off on the end, your opponent wins one-half of the pot. But if you make the flush the first time around, then he has another chance to beat you on the second deal. Then those cards are taken away and the dealer burns and turns, burns and turns again, and then you figure out who won on the second deal.

Obviously, if you do insurance on fifth street only, you burn and turn only one card, but you are still playing for a half of the pot. Sometimes, they will run the deal three times, by burning and turning three times in a row. In this case, you have a chance to win one-third of the pot each time.

Insurance is fairly common in pot-limit poker, depending on who the players are, whether they like to gamble, and so on. The guy with the best hand makes the main decisions — he makes an offer, and if his opponent wants to go with the deal they do insurance, and if his opponent doesn't want it they don't do it. The leader doesn't have to offer insurance at all if he prefers to gamble with the hand.

I remember one time when I was playing pot-limit hold'em against Betty Carey. On fourth street the board showed K-J-8-5. I had kings and jacks and she had kings and fives with one card to come. The odds were 21-to-1 in my favor. Betty says, "I'll give you fourteen." Without even thinking I answer, "No, I'm not gonna take that low a price." We had $18,000 in the pot. If I had taken insurance at 14-to-1 at $2,000, that means I would have gotten $28,000, so I would be winner to the pot anyhow. But I said no ... and she caught a five on the end!

When you stop to think about it, insurance sometimes is well worth your taking it. Anytime you can get big odds, you probably should take it because, as Murphy's Law goes, "Anything that can happen will happen." Just ask me!

In the Carey deal, I couldn't lose: Either way, insurance or not, I would have won money even though I would have had to give up a little bit. As it turned out I got nothing and she won the whole pot.

T. J.'s parents, Jane and Bill Cloutier, join T. J. and Joy as he accepts the trophy for winning the $500 buy-in no-limit hold'em tournament at the Super Bowl of Poker in 1986.

STARTING HANDS

The best starting hands in pot-limit Omaha are:
(1) A-J-A-10 double suited, and other premium high
    hands with aces and two connectors;
(2) A-A-K-K and other hands with aces and a big pair;
(3) Rundown hands that have four connecting cards;
(4) Two bare aces without connectors (for a minimum
    bet); and
(5) Two bare kings without connectors (for a minimum
    bet).

Big Pairs with Connectors

Although the computer says that the best hand to start with is A-K-A-K double suited, I think that is wrong. In my opinion, the best starting hand is A-J-A-10 double suited. You can make only one straight with A-K-A-K, but you can make several straights with the A-J-A-10.

With the A-J-A-10 you still have the nut flush possibility. You don't get this hand very often, but when you get it you have a lot more possibilities with it than with the A-K-A-K.

The Middle Rundowns such as:

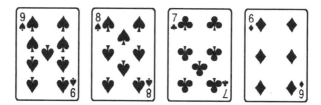

The Big Rundowns such as:

The Small Rundowns such as:

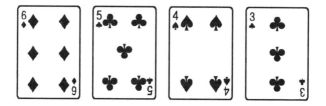

Rundown hands are major hands in pot-limit Omaha. If it's a small rundown hand such as 6-5-4-3, the only time being suited comes into play is when you're heads up. If you're playing a multiway pot where there's any action someone usually has a bigger flush draw than you.

The rundowns are great pick-off hands. If you've studied your opponents, you know that *this* guy raises with aces and *that* guy calls with big suited connectors. Now they're both in the pot and you have cards like 7-6-5-4 in your hand. You say to yourself, "If the flop comes with any babies or middle cards, I've got it." So you might play this type of hand — I do and it's been very successful for me over the years. You don't want to play heads up with these types of hands, though, so you wouldn't call a big raise with them against a single opponent. Suppose you flop two pair and you know the other guy has aces, and the board makes two pair that aren't your two pair — you're a goner. And you can really get involved with these types of hands.

Another hand to play is three rundown cards with a pair (8-8-7-6, 7-7-6-5, 9-8-7-7, and so on).

If you know you're up against a big pair and you flop one of your middle cards along with a straight draw, you'll have by far the best hand. If they're playing big cards and your eight flops, that eight probably doesn't work with their hands so that their straight possibilities probably aren't there either (unless they backdoor them). So, almost any type of three-card rundown with a pair can be a good hand to play.

I said *almost* — forget about playing hands like 4-3-2-2. The danger is in set-over-set situations, and you usually can't flop the nut straight with a hand like that. If you play those little hands at all, it's usually from the blind in an unraised pot or from very late position for a minimum bet.

The Dangerous Dangler

The cardinal rule for rundown hands is this: Never play a hand that has a dangler in it. Don't let hands like Q-J-10-6 or K-Q-J-4 entice you into playing a pot.

A three-card rundown with a dangler:

A big pair with one connector and a dangler:

Suppose you have K♥ K♣ Q♠ 3♦. You have three big cards working together and one oddball out there dangling off the roof. You usually *don't* play this hand. These types of hands can get you in a lot of trouble. Even if the dangler is suited, if it is *not* suited to an ace, it is still a dangler. "But in reality," Tom adds, "there are a lot of players who will call a minimum bet from late position with this hand."

A Tip from the Top
Don't play a hand with a dangler in it.

Playing a hand with a single gap and a pair — 10-8-8-7 or 9-9-7-6 or similar hands — is reasonable, but never play three-holers such as 10-9-5-4.

Any hand with three or more gaps in it makes the fourth card a dangler. If you make a straight with it, it never is the nuts. With two gaps (Q-Q-J-8, for example), you can sometimes make the nuts. I'm not going to play this type of hand in a raised pot because it is marginal. I might play it against one man from out back for a raise if I knew that the pot definitely would be heads-up, but I wouldn't play Q-Q-J-6 for a raise ... there's that dangler again.

The Small Rundowns

The small rundown hands are topped by the seven on down: 7-6-5-4, 6-5-4-3, 6-5-5-4. I wouldn't suggest playing them in tournaments, but in side action the small rundown hands can be profitable. If you're getting three-way action or more on a hand in a raised pot and you can put your opponents on big hands, sometimes it's nice to call a raise with a small rundown hand because sometimes you can take them off because you know you're the only one playing them. In other words, you know your cards are live.

If you don't hit the flop, you throw the hand away, but a lot of times the flop will come with a small pair and then you've made a set against an overpair. And quite often, you'll make a straight or two pair on the flop. And if you've put someone on two aces, that's great.

"T. J. is saying that even if you call a small raise before the flop," Tom adds, "when you're getting a price to it multi-way *and* you know where your opponents are at in the hand, you may very well have a very live hand ... and a lot of times they're trying to pick each other apart. Sure, you're spotting them the aces and the kings but you're getting a price for a live hand. Obviously, if the flop doesn't hit you, you're done with it but if it does hit you, you can bust some of these people.

"Many times I'll play the small rundowns, knowing that I'm probably up against aces, when I really know where they're at. I know they have the best cards, but I'll take the chance to outflop them with my live cards.

"In tournament play you have less reason to speculate with these kinds of hands in raised pots because your opponents can put a lot of pressure on you. Therefore, you're less likely to want to play them in pot-limit tournaments than you are in ring games."

Playing Two Aces

It is a big fallacy to raise with aces, not get any help on the flop, and get broke to the hand. Some players will have $2,000 in front of them, get $1,000 in before the flop, see it come with 8-5-4, and move in with their aces. This is a bad move. If they get called, they're either beat or are a huge dog. They could be against a set, a straight, two pair, or a huge wraparound drawing hand.

Suppose you have isolated an opponent in pot-limit Omaha and you know that he has aces. Sometimes, you will flop one pair, and even though you know that you're up against aces, you also realize that if you double-pair you'll win the pot. Of course, if the board pairs a card that isn't in your hand, the aces will take the pot with top two pair, but if it doesn't pair, you've got him. So, a lot of players will take off after somebody with aces if they just make one pair on the flop. I've done it a zillion times when I *knew* that my opponent had either aces or kings.

Playing Two Kings

Suppose you're dealt two kings double-suited. This is *not* a raising hand unless you're way around back (in a very late position). The reason it's not a raising hand is because if you get reraised you know that you're an underdog in the hand. But I see so many people make the mistake of raising with two kings, getting reraised, and calling the reraise.

What are you hoping to accomplish with this hand? You're just hoping to catch a king on the flop, but you're a dog to start with and, if you know that aces are out, the kings are in big trouble. "Even if you have a pair of kings double-suited and you make the flush, if your opponent raises when you bet, you can be pretty sure that you're looking at the nut flush," Tom adds.

In pot-limit Omaha, then, a pair of kings is usually a piece of junk if an opponent is willing to put all his money in before the flop. In that case, you know that you're up against aces because any nit worth his salt is going to dog his hand unless he has aces.

Some players will raise limpers with K♠ K♦ 5♦ 4♥ from, say, sixth position with two players behind them. We don't recommend this play. If the raiser gets reraised he can use that hand for toilet paper! "I virtually would never raise with two kings and weak side cards against two limpers," Tom notes.

Remember that reraises in pot-limit Omaha are 90 percent aces, and if it's a good player reraising, it's aces with suits. As Tom says, "A good player may call with a hand such as A-A-9-8 with one or no suits, but he probably won't put all his money in before the flop unless his hand is much stronger than that."

But do you know where you *might* raise with two kings in pot-limit Omaha? In the little blind and the big blind ... and hope that you don't get reraised. And possibly from the button (or very late position) *into* the two blinds, with the idea of mucking the hand if either of them is willing to push it all in.

Trap Hands

You can lose a lot of money if you get caught with the second-best hand. Tom adds that trap hands usually consist of kings and queens in raised pots. Queens double-suited, for example, can put you in a world of misery. King or queen-high flush draws are other types of trap hands that are even worse in pot-limit Omaha than in the limit version.

Position and Hand Selection

"Position isn't as important as starting hand selection *before* the flop in pot-limit Omaha," Tom starts off. He's right, but once the flop is out there, position *is* important.

The thing that is *really* important about position is this: If you play a hand, can you stand a raise with it? Whether or not people are willing to stand a raise with hands such as medium rundowns (8-7-6-5) dictates whether they will play those types of hands from up front. I'm willing to stand a small raise with them so I'll play them.

So long as you don't raise coming in and there's only a single raise behind you, that raise usually isn't so big that you can't call it because the game is pot-limit and that format dictates how much anybody can raise. Tom adds, "In tournaments, position is somewhat more important and allows you to put on a little more pressure because people can't go back into their pockets, but still, the value of your starting hands is far more important than position."

Raising Before the Flop

If you like to raise in pot-limit Omaha, my advice is that the only hands worth raising are aces with connectors and suits *or* big connecting cards (A-K-Q-J). And even medium rundown hands are better hands to raise with than kings. If you put a man on aces, you don't want to have an ace in your hand: Aceless rundown hands such as K-Q-J-10 are what you want. You don't mind if he catches an ace on the flop because *you* need one.

With the K-Q-J-10, you'd like to see the flop come something like A-Q-10 because it makes a straight for you and if your opponent has pocket aces, you're likely to get a lot of action on the hand. Just remember that if you have an ace in your hand and one comes on the flop with the connectors that you're looking for, you'll make two aces and he'll make three of them if he started with aces.

You don't raise with kings, you don't raise with queens, and you don't raise with jacks in pot-limit Omaha. I'm not saying that you don't take a flop to these hands when you have connecting cards with them — but you don't raise with them. You're hoping to hit something on the flop but why put a lot of money in with them? If one overcard comes to your pair, you're often in trouble.

A Tip from the Top
Almost no hand is worth raising preflop.

"Practically no hand is worth raising preflop because people will know where you're at and they will play accordingly, while you won't know for sure where they're at," Tom explains. "This is especially true in tournaments."

That's right. If you're playing in a ring game, people will raise with aces because they're playing differently than they would play in tournaments and they will raise with a lot of different hands. With aces, you're always trying to narrow it down to one other player and yourself if you can.

"When you raise, most players are already thinking that you have aces or something close to them, unless you're the type of player who regularly raises with rundowns," Tom reasons. Of course, playing your aces when somebody has raised in front of you is a different story. Many times, you can put enough pressure on the pot to blow everybody away and sometimes even get the raiser to lay down his hand. So, you can win it right there or at least get it heads up with the original raiser with what you know is the best hand.

PLAYING ON THE FLOP

"It's all in the flip of the flop" Tom muses. "Once you see the flop, remember that you have seen seven of the nine cards from which you will make your final hand. Your big decisions are made on the flop, even more so that in the forms of two-card hold'em, because you have so much more information right there in front of you."

A lot more flops are seen in pot-limit Omaha and a lot fewer rivers are seen (unless all the money goes into the pot on the flop). With four cards in each hand, you'll find more multiway pots in Omaha than in hold'em. In pot-limit, multi-way pots are usually three or four-handed.

"A lot of people will call a modest raise to see the flop," Tom explains, "and then fold on the flop. If three or four people have called a raise before the flop, the pot is pretty big and they would have to flop a really big hand in order to be able to afford to continue. At that point, they can't play a marginal drawing hand." Generally, when the river is seen in pot-limit Omaha, all the money is usually already in the pot ... that is, if it's a big pot.

Top Two Pair

If you have top two pair or bottom set and you get heavy action, generally speaking you're a gone goose. You're either up against a gigantic drawing hand, which is a favorite, or a made hand such as a higher set that has you beat.

It's very easy to get away from bottom set in a multiway pot, but it's not so easy in a heads-up pot. In hold'em the board might come 7-8-9 and you have Q-J in your hand, two overcards and a middle buster ... you might take a shot with this hand. But in pot-limit Omaha, you'd never take a shot with it. In the hold'em example, if you put your opponent on having a pair of one of the board cards, you might call if you have two overcards with a middle buster straight draw. You have 20 ways to win — you have four tens, three jacks and three queens, which is ten wins twice (since you have fourth and fifth streets both to come) — and with those 20 wins you're approximately a 7-to-5 dog.

In Omaha there are so many backdoor possibilities that are unseen. A lot of times, you'll raise the pot with a hand like A-A-10-9 and you'll wind up winning the pot with the 10-9, not the aces. So many times, it isn't the primary cards that you win with in Omaha, it's your secondary cards.

Flopping A Set

I've played a zillion Omaha hands where I flopped a set, another guy flopped a set, and a third player had a big draw against us (such as a straight or a flush draw). When that happens, a lot of times the sets are gone south for the winter, they're dead. This is another reason why the game is so treacherous, why you have to play so carefully, and why the better players will get the money over the long run. They can get away from hands that other people won't give up. They'll know to lay down that set or that nine-high straight when they can't get any bigger or have no backdoor possibilities.

Ideally, you want to flop a good hand and have a draw that could improve it even further. For example, suppose you have 10♠ 10♣ 9♦ 8♠ and the flop comes 10♥ 7♠ 6♣ . You couldn't get a bigger flop: You have the nut straight and top set. You could fill up and win if someone else has a lower set. If an opponents fills up, he won't win because you'll fill up higher. These hands do come up — they sound like they're from Outer Mongolia but they come up all the time in Omaha.

Straights and Flushes

Suppose you flop the nut straight with no possibility of improving, and two of a suit also come on the flop. This can be a dangerous situation for you. You would like to have another draw when you flop a straight — maybe also a flop to a flush draw or an even higher straight. A nice time to make the nut straight is on the end, or on fourth street where you can get enough money in to blow your opponents out of it. But on the flop, you can't get enough money in to blow them out of there so you might want to play this hand softly.

Another thing that a lot of people do is this: They have a nut flush draw on the flop and if you bet into them, they will empty their whole stack to draw to that flush. I don't think this is a good play to make. "Sometimes they do it as a semibluff," Tom says, "to try to blow you away." Sure, they might blow you away with a big raise, but there's less bluffing going on in pot-limit Omaha than you would think.

A Tip from the Top
Most of the time, somebody's peddling the nuts.

You see, pot-limit Omaha is a game in which you're peddling the nuts a great percentage of the time. If a guy who's a player is swinging at you in a pot, you can pretty well figure that he has the nuts, whatever the nuts can be at that point. So you take that into consideration. If you have a couple of draws to make the bigger nuts, then it's up to you whether you want to play or fold.

"Unlike other games such as pot-limit hold'em in which, if you have the nuts you try to trap," Tom adds, "in pot-limit Omaha you peddle the nuts as fast as you can right on the flop. You don't give free cards unless you've flopped something gigantic, like quads." That's right. I'd hate to count how many times I've flopped the nut flush and given one card off and the board paired on the turn. Then you have to slow down to a walk and pray that your opponent hasn't filled up.

It takes years and years to learn all the little nuances of play in this game. Every time you play it, you'll learn something different and the players are all going to be different and play in many different ways.

Bottom Two Pair

Bottom two pair in Omaha is absolutely nothing. You don't lead with bottom two pair in Omaha unless you put a player who has reraised the pot on aces or kings. There's a big difference between doing that and (incorrectly) leading against anything else.

Suppose you're playing against one man and you put him on kings or aces. If you flop bottom two pair, you can go after this guy because it is very likely that you have the best hand. But if you have top pair/bottom pair or bottom two pair in a *multiway* pot, you have to be very, very careful with them. If you get any action, somebody usually has a set, top two pair, or top and bottom pair. Those bottom two pair are bad cards. If you fill up, you think you have a hand but you don't have anything — somebody usually has a bigger full house.

Bluffing

"There are some times when you can bluff in pot-limit Omaha" Tom explains. "Specifically, if you have the lone ace of spades in your hand and three spades hit on the flop, you know that nobody can have the nut flush. Sometimes you can run people off in this situation." That's true, but you'd better try that play against good players. Never try it against a weak player because he will call you with that small flush for all your money.

Everybody knows the "lone ace" play when three of a suit are on the board. So, a lot of times good players will chop you off when you try to make the play, and other times they will fold, but bad players never throw *anything* away. If they have a flush, they're calling. Also, you shouldn't overwork this play against good players. And if you do win the pot with that lone ace, you never show it ... just throw your cards away. Don't let them know that you even know the play. You never want to show a hand if you don't have to.

When I won the pot-limit Omaha title at the Four Queens, it was down to Slim and me. I had a jack-high flush and I knew that I had the best hand. When three clubs came on the flop, Slim moved in. I beat him into the pot with my flush — he had a 10-high flush. But I knew I had the best hand; my instincts told me so. I wouldn't make that play very often, but Slim has a way of talking ... he talked one way when he had a hand and he talked another way when his hand was weaker. And you know, he's talking all the time, so you just have to pick up on the intonation of his voice and what he's saying. In the two pots that he had beaten Mansour Matloubi and Mike Sexton for all their money, I knew that Slim had a hand ... I wasn't in the pot but I *knew* he had the hand. And I used that information to beat him when we got heads-up.

It all goes back to knowing your opponents. Brunson talks about the importance of having recall. In his opinion, the thing that makes a poker player great is his ability to recall, maybe not what that exact player has done, but what that over-all class of players has done in past situations. Doyle works with classes of players, I work with individual players. I have total recall on players and situations. I don't know why I have that knack ... I'll forget lots of things (I've even forgotten my book-writing appointments when I was out on the golf course), but I don't forget how a person plays.

Yesterday I was playing in a $40-$80 game and this guy that I'd never seen play before played his hand exactly the same way every time. He always played check-raise on the flop every time he had a hand. So I tell myself, "I'm never gonna bet when this guy's in the pot with me. I'll never bet without having a huge hand because I know he's gonna raise me." You use that kind of information to your advantage.

I've been in situations with Tom where I could have told you exactly which two cards he had. "Yes," Tom defends himself, "but I've also known when you were making a move at me and I called you. The classic example was at the Commerce hold'em tournament earlier this year. I raised with A-J and you put all your money in on a reraise. I thought about it for less than two seconds and called because I knew you were making a play. As it turns out, you had a suited K-J, caught runner-runner to make a flush, and broke me! But I was dead right ... I had you exactly where I wanted you. I was dead right and got dead broke!"

Continuing with our conversation, I reminded Tom that I had him dead right when he had the A-8 and I had the two queens in the finals of another tournament. "Sure, you suckered me into making a play when you had a real hand" Tom said. "Sometimes a guy can make the right play at the wrong time, you know."

Yes, that's true and there's not a thing you can do about it. "But I lucked out that time," Tom added. "I snagged an ace to win the tournament!"

When There's Action on the Flop

If you get action on the flop, keep in mind that a lot of the cards you need to make your hand might be gone already. In a nine-handed Omaha game, 36 cards are out before the flop, and one card is burned making 37 cards out. That leaves 15 cards in play. (Actually, you count it as 16 because the burn is a random card.) A lot of the cards you need to make your hand are already out and you have to take that into consideration. (In my opinion, the game should be played seven-handed so that there's more of a deck to play with.)

Now let's take a look at a situation in which you've raised before the flop with a premium hand and you don't catch the flop that you had hoped for.

You've started with the best hand possible, A-A-J-10 double-suited, and there's a lot of money in the pot.

The flop comes:

What do you do? You're gone ... you fold.

Now suppose the flop comes:

You have top two pair, but you don't have a straight draw. How do you play this hand? Carefully! Obviously, you've raised before the flop. If you get any action, somebody might already have the straight, and somebody else might have a set. The top two pair isn't necessarily the best hand. You're not as worried about somebody having a K-Q draw at the top straight because you have two of their straight cards with your two aces. Obviously, you've raised before the flop and these people are giving you credit for having aces. If they play the hand, the idea that you have two aces has gone through their mind and they know that two of their outs are gone, so the K-Q might not be the hand that's playing against you.

The Idiot End of the Straight. Now let's say that you have 7-7-6-4 in your hand and the flop comes with 9-8-2. You never draw to this hand. If four fives are remaining in the deck, all you're hoping to do is catch one of them. If a 10 comes on the turn, you're usually up against a top-end straight. You don't draw to the idiot end of the straight. If you ask me if I've ever done it — yes I have. And have I won big pots with it? Yes I have. And was I lucky to be winner? Very lucky! And have I lost with it? Yes I have.

It's similar to counting in blackjack. Some people use a basic count, some have a very advanced counting system, and others use a super-advanced count system. It just shows you which players you can do things against, see what I'm saying? The basic count will never win as much as the super count does, so don't take as many chances with it. You have to know your own skill level and who you're playing against. Because you can get absolutely murdered in pot-limit Omaha.

The Wraparound Hands

I recently stood a raise in a cash game with 9-9-8-7. The board came 7-6-2 and no suits. A guy led off with a decent bet and I called him. All I had was an open end straight, but I had the top end of it (and I had the top pair), so it looked like I might win the pot if I could double-pair. And if I could make the straight on either end I could win the pot. Plus, he was a pretty loose player. So I called, made the straight on the turn, and won a nice pot. But if I'd gotten big action in this hand I probably wouldn't have played it because all I had was an open-end straight draw, not a wraparound.

Having a wraparound makes a big difference. Say the flop comes 10-7-2 and you have J-9-8-6 in your hand. That's a complete wrap — you can catch a card on either end or in the middle and make your hand. Now suppose the flops comes J-10-2 and you have K-Q-9-8. You can catch any card on either end, or one of your own cards, to make your hand. We call it "Maine to Spain." That's a big *big* hand.

The Inside Wrap. There's also what is called an "inside wrap." Suppose the flop comes with A-10-4 and you have K-Q-J-9 in your hand. You have an *inside* wrap. Or if you have a K-Q-9-6 and the flop comes J-10-4, you have a three-card *outside* wrap. If you get a big draw like this on the flop are you going to push it? Sometimes. It depends on what you're up against. A lot of times, if you know by his actions that a player has top set, you're done with it on fourth street if you don't catch your card. You might be a favorite on third street, but if you miss it on the turn you're a dog.

A lot of players will play that hand very aggressively on the flop, commit themselves, so they can't be blown out if they don't make it on fourth street. Or they might make a pot-sized bet that will double the price that it costs other players to go for their draws. If somebody comes out on fourth street with a big bet and you haven't made it, you have to make the decision, "Do I want to try to make this hand?" If you haven't led to this hand or you haven't raised so that you don't have a lot of money invested in the hand, you can get away from it now at a fairly cheap price. You have to give yourself that option — and that's why you often don't lead with this hand.

A complete wrap with no suits on the board — that's a hand you'll go to war with quite often. Many times, you will commit enough money on the flop to ensure that you're going to see two cards. Sometimes, it all depends on how you're running and other factors like that. It shouldn't matter, but somehow it does. Just because you've lost five hands in a row doesn't mean that you're going to lose the sixth one. The odds never change, the odds on the sixth hand are the same as they were on the first one. But you don't feel the same about it — nobody ever does.

Logically, what's the difference if you've lost five hands in a row? If you've played them right and you didn't get there, so what? Whatever the odds are of your making the sixth hand, they are still intact, they don't change. Just because you've lost a few hands in a row doesn't change things downward to being even money when you are a 2-to-1 favorite.

Slowplaying

Is there a time when you slowplay big hands from up front? Or when you try a check-raise? Usually not. You can't give free cards in Omaha because there are too many ways of making a hand.

"I really believe that very strongly," Tom agrees. "I think that it's a huge mistake. When players who have been playing a lot of pot-limit hold'em move to pot-limit Omaha, you'll see them making the mistake of using slowplay tactics to try to trap people. In Omaha, there are so many people holding "backdoor hands" who wouldn't call the flop if you bet. But you don't bet and suddenly they catch a magic card that gives them a flush draw or a straight draw or a set or this and that, so now they're going to play.

"Therefore, if the flop comes with a 5-4-3 and you have 9-8-7-6, you are *not* going to slowplay it on the flop. You're better off firing and hoping that someone has enough of a hand to come after you. If they raise you and there are no suits on board, you like that."

Tom's right, but I'd feel a lot better doing it with the nut flush than with a straight. We've already told you that you can throw hands away if there's a lot of action when you flop the nut straight, and that's why this example works better with the nut flush. If you check your nut flush and the board pairs, you can be in a lot of trouble. You're not necessarily in a *lot* of trouble, but you would play it *as though* you are. "Once the boards pairs and you have a straight or flush," adds Tom, "you can't play with any real confidence."

What's really interesting about this game is that if there's any action at all, good players will throw their hands away when they flop a set *and* the flop also comes with three of a suit. But the weaker players — and there are some who play this game — know only that they've flopped a set. "I've got a set," they say to themselves, "and I don't care if the other guy has a flush ... I'm gonna pair this hand and beat him." And sometimes they do, but in the long run they're going to lose their money.

A Tip from the Top
When you have it, bet it!

If you flop the nut flush, you *bet* the nut flush. You don't slowplay, you play very straightforwardly. If you have it, you bet it. But that's not a cut-and-dried rule. Let me tell you why: There are players who play two pair like they were four of a kind. You have watched them and you know that they will bet two pair or a set on the flop with three-of-a suit on the board. You might slowplay against that type of player; you might just flat call. You're taking a chance that the board won't pair, but you know that you're playing against a very aggressive player who will bet again and commit himself to the pot.

"There are some other hands you can consider slow playing. If you flop the top set with the nut flush draw, you might slowplay," Tom suggests. Yes, but sometimes leading with those hands creates bigger pots. Suppose somebody else bets into you when you have top set and the nut flush draw on the flop. You're not going to raise him right there. For example, say that you have a K-Q-Q-J with one suit and the flop comes Q-10-9. You have top set and the straight. This is a good example of when you can give a free card, provided there isn't a suit out there.

"But what if it also comes with two of your suit?" Tom asks. "Then you'd have the nut straight but only a second-nut flush draw." I don't know, Tom, Columbus took a chance — I might! This is the type of hand that if someone bets into you, you might smooth call *because* you have an extra out. A lot of times, there are guys who will flop two pair or a set when the flop comes with three of a suit and they'll lead out. If they get called, a lot of times they'll shut down. They'll bet once to see if their hand is any good and then they'll shut down. Then you'll have to bet it on fourth street and leave it up to them as to whether they want to go any further with it. If you have an opponent who's stuck and plowin', he'll come. You hope that's the guy's who's in the pot with you.

Does the flop thin out the field? Yes, it usually does but you still see a lot of multiway pots. A lot of times, a ton of money goes in on the flop if any hands are out there — and in Omaha, there usually is something out there every time! But you'd better have the nuts or the nut draw if you call on the flop. If you draw, you'd better be drawing to the nuts.

Suppose somebody bets in front of you, there are two hearts on the board, and you have the K♥ Q♥. Your question is, "Since one of my opponents might have the ace-high flush draw, why should I call?" But if *you* have the ace-high flush draw plus some other outs, that's a different story.

As I've said, I don't want to sacrifice all my chips on a one-type draw such as a flush draw in which you have nine outs twice, 18, if none of those cards are already gone. If you have an open-end straight draw, you have eight outs twice, 16. If you have a wraparound straight draw, you don't have much of a decision to make: You're going to play.

A Tip from the Top
To continue playing past the flop,
either have the boss hand or a draw to it.

Either flop the nuts or have a draw to it. Remember that 90 percent of the time in Omaha, players are peddling the nuts. They may not be peddling them in a heads-up situation, that's when the hands might be a little weaker. But in any multiway pot, somebody's drawing at the nuts if they don't already have it.

PLAYING ON THE TURN

The action usually thins down to two or three players on the turn, although you can't really tell since every pot is different. But if there has been any action on the flop, the field usually will be thinned down to just two or three players. Very seldom would you have more than three players left if there has been a bet on the flop. Usually, if you make the nuts on the turn you bet it. And if anyone bets into you, you usually will raise it.

Of course, there are occasions when you don't raise it. For example, when you make the nut full house or four of a kind, these hands are big enough that you can actually give a free card. "But straights and flushes usually are not big enough to give a free card because there's always the possibility that you're up against a set that your opponent might fill on the river," Tom adds. "Say that you were on a draw and you've made your hand on fourth street. Now you want to protect it. The pot usually is big enough that you have a chance of doing exactly that with a pot-sized bet. If someone does decide to call you when you have the nuts, they have made a mistake, no matter what their draw is. If you have the nuts on fourth street you're the favorite with one card to come, so you want to protect your hand at all costs."

**A Tip from the Top
Pot-limit Omaha is not a free-card game!
That's the cardinal rule.**

If you make your draw on the turn, you bet it. Just as you don't usually give free cards on the flop you don't give them going into fifth street either. If you make it, bet it.

"Don't forget that if you have called your opponent on the flop with a drawing hand, and the card that makes your hand comes on the turn, your opponent is going to be fearful that that card may have made your hand," Tom explains. "So, he's usually not going to bet it for you. To put it another way, when you have the nuts, don't expect your opponent to bet it for you. Everybody is aware that the nuts can be out there, so when a card comes that can make the nuts for someone, a lot of times they will shut down, even with a fairly strong hand. You'll just have to do your own betting most of the time."

If your opponent is first to act and he led at the pot on the flop, he's not going to bet it for you on the turn ... he's going to check to you. He might fold when you bet ... or he might not. Remember that he had something that he was leading at to start with. Since he checked to you, he has to call only one bet to see the river whereas if he had bet into you and you had raised, he would have had to call a whole lot more to see the last card. If it's an unraised pot that isn't too big, he might decide to try to beat you on the river. You welcome these types of players because they will have to draw out on you to beat you. Of course, in Omaha they *do* draw out on you a lot.

When You Backdoor a Hand

Backdoor draws are ones that you don't recognize quite as often. Suppose the flop comes with two hearts and a club. You bet on the flop and your opponent calls — he's on a heart draw. Then on fourth street comes a second club. He may be double-suited in hearts and clubs and now has two flush draws, so he's probably going to play with you.

When you make a backdoor flush that isn't the nuts, it is less likely that the nut flush is out against you. A backdoor flush can be weaker, and it has much more value. That's another reason why this game can be so treacherous: A player can start off drawing at one hand and end up drawing at another hand. It's amazing how many times you'll see the flop come with two of a suit and wind up with three of the second suit on the board at the river.

"If there's any action on fourth street, there's a far greater danger of someone backing into another draw (such as a flush that he wasn't originally drawing to) to go along with his primary draw that he called with on the flop," Tom explains. "If I'm the receiver of the runner-runner flush, I'll often bet it even if it isn't the nuts." Runner-runner has killed more Omaha games than anything else. Amen.

Berry Johnston and Tom McEvoy at the final table of the 1992 World Series of Poker limit high Omaha championship event.

PLAYING AT THE RIVER

"A lot of times there will be two or three players left at the river," Tom says. "You have to be careful if there are two or more people besides yourself contesting the pot. Just because there was only one club on the flop when you made your nut straight doesn't mean that someone couldn't have made a flush on the river if it happens to come runner-runner clubs. It's far more likely in an Omaha game than it is in a hold'em game. If you did flop the nut straight and two running clubs popped out, then you must play very cautiously at the river." Of course, if you have the nuts, you *want* all nine players there with you.

There are times when bad things happen to good hands at the river. Let me tell you a story along this line. I took a half of Bill Duarte (a very good player who we call "Boston Billy") in a real big ring game that Phil Hellmuth and Tony Dee and all those guys were playing in down at Oceanside. It got down to the three of them and Billy had the A♦ 10♦ 9♠ 8♠ in his hand. They made a little raise to come in and he called. The flop came with the 7♦ 6♣ 5♦. He flopped the stone joint three-handed and he was drawing at the stone joint with the nut flush draw.

Tony Dee led off and made a big bet at the pot. Phil moved in and Billy called for all his chips. This pot had almost $30,000 in it and Phil was flat sizzlin'. Here are the hands that were out against Billy: Phil had the K♦ 3♦, the second-nut flush draw and nothing else. Tony had a jack-high flush draw in diamonds and the K♣ 7♣. He paired the seven on the flop, which is what he took off betting with. Then all this money went in.

On fourth street the board pairs the seven and now Tony has trip sevens. Phil's completely out of it, drawing dead. On

111

fifth street comes the K♠. Tony caught a seven on the turn to make trip sevens and a king on the end to make a full house! We lost this $30,000 pot where we had one man drawing dead and the other one drawing to two running cards for all the money. You can't get your money in any better than that. This just shows you what *can* happen in pot-limit games.

Tom brings up an interesting point: "If the scenario had been slightly different with the 7-6-5 flop — for example, some players went to the center before it got to you and the board had two suited cards that weren't your suit — you would have to give serious thought to passing this hand."

That's true but you might consider playing it more often in a three-handed game than you would in a full ring because there are so many cards that aren't going to be coming out with only three players in the game. In the shorthanded situation, more than half the deck is never going to be in play, but when you're playing in a full ring most of the cards are out every time and the hands that can be made are going to be easier to make. When there's a stub with half of the deck left, the cards that your opponents need to make their hands might never come into play because they might all be buried in the deck. I don't know if you've thought of it that way, but it's something to consider.

When You Miss at the River

Would you try a bluff at the pot if you miss everything you've been drawing to at the river? At the river the pot is usually pretty big, so you're talking about sacrificing a lot of money to bluff on the end. It's hard to think of a situation where I'd want to take the chance of losing a lot more money, a pot-sized bet. One of the top European players I've watched used to like to try bluffing on the end, but I've seen him get picked off so many times it'll make your head spin. If they know you'll bluff, they *will* call you.

You have to be a very strong player and know that your opponent also had been drawing and had missed his hand before you would try a bluff. We've all bluffed in our poker careers, but in the long run I think it's a bad idea to be bluffing at the river. I just can't see trying it unless you can absolutely put a man on a big draw that he has missed.

Why? Because a lot of money has been committed to the pot by then and most of these guys will call you so fast it'll make your head spin. When you're drawing, the other man usually isn't drawing ... he has a hand if he's a player.

The only time when you might be able to bluff at the river is when a card comes that will allow you to represent a hand. For example, a flush card comes. Maybe there were two flush cards on the flop and you've put your opponent on a set. If the third flush card comes at the river, you might take a shot at the pot. But you'd better know where you're at because you can get yourself called in a New York minute. A player might say to himself, "He's got the lone ace working and he's just trying to pull that lone-ace play on me," and then he'll call you. And if you're wrong in your evaluation of his hand, you'll lose all that money that you bet on the end. Sometimes you just have to suck it up and take a loss, take your medicine and move on to the next hand.

A lot of people think that the bluff is a big part of all poker games, but Omaha isn't really a bluffing game and that's the first thing you have to consider when you start thinking about trying a bluff. Again, Omaha is a "peddling-the-nuts" game. There are certain situations in which you can bluff, but your win percentage at bluffing in Omaha is a lot lower than it is in hold'em. And in limit high Omaha, you can hardly ever run a successful bluff.

One more point here: Get in the habit of never showing your cards when you win a pot (and haven't been called on the final bet).

Check-Raising on the End

Do you ever check-raise at the river? Probably the only time you would ever check-raise at the river is when you're playing against a super-aggressive player. You have to *know* that he's going to bet at the river. Most of the time in Omaha a guy will shut down if he has been betting a big hand and fifth street damages him a little bit so that there might be bigger hands out. In this case, you might as well bet and put him to the test of whether or not he wants to call the bet. If you're playing the hand for a check-raise, you probably will lose the money you would have won if you had bet on the end.

How often do you have to lay down a hand at the river? It isn't a good practice to have to lay it down at the river, but you might have been in there with a monster double-draw and miss everything at the end. Then you just lay it down — what else can you do? I can't think of any other reason why you'd go to the river and then throw away your hand.

A Bad Beat at the River

I was in a game at Tunica one weekend not long ago with a guy from Kentucky and we're playing $25-$50-$100 blinds. I had A-Q-Q-10 suited in hearts. The flop came Q-7-3 with two hearts. I had the nut flush draw and I had top set. I liked the hand.

I bet on the flop and he raised me. I raised him back and he called the reraise. On fourth street came an offsuit deuce. I took the lead. I had $27,000 in front of me before the hand started and I put it all in the pot. He called me.

On fifth street came the five of spades — and he showed me a seven-high straight! He had a 6-4 in his hand. His flush draw was no good, my top set already had the pot won on the flop, and I lose $27,000 on this one hand where he had three fives in the whole deck that he could win with.

He was on a suicide mission in this hand — he'd been on one most of the day, which is how he got stuck in the first place. His girlfriend would bring over these packets of $10,000 each and he'd take two or three at a time from her and put them on the table.

I almost dropped out of my seat when that five came. I'll never forget it. We were playing triple-draw lowball and pot-limit Omaha and I was $17,000 winner when this hand started. I could've gone to Lloyd's of London and gotten 100-to-1 on my hand after the flop. You can peddle the nuts but you can still lose.

"Did you go home?" Tom asked.

"No, I went to the craps table." ♣

Chapter 4

LIMIT HIGH OMAHA

by Tom McEvoy
Commentary by T. J. Cloutier

Limit high Omaha was once described as "the game of the future." Its popularity as a casino game peaked in the mid '80s and has been steadily declining. Although it is an action game that many players enjoy, limit high Omaha has been eclipsed in interest by the even more action-packed split version, Omaha high-low. Some people believe that it is the volatility of limit high Omaha that has led to its demise, that too many players were going broke playing it, but I disagree. Limit high Omaha isn't spread at very high limits so people don't usually get broke playing the game. About the biggest game I've seen spread is $20-$40 and very few people are going to lose the ranch playing those limits.

What I'm saying is that limit high Omaha is not a bankroll buster — leave that distinction to pot-limit Omaha. People like games with lots of action and they often find a lot of excuses to play a ton of pots in limit high Omaha. They justify playing too many hands — a big mistake — and that is a major reason why this exciting action game has gained a certain degree of notoriety as a bankroll buster.

If you like to play high Omaha, and if you play it well, there is no reason why you cannot become a winner. In this chapter, T. J. and I will be discussing some strategies that we believe will take you to the winner's circle.

General Comments

Position is less important in limit high Omaha than it is in hold'em because there are more playable hands. Blind stealing shouldn't even be in your repertoire. There is very little blind stealing in all forms of Omaha, but in limit high Omaha it is practically nonexistent. Because there are so many playable four-card combinations, you have to play pretty much on the merits of your hand. You have to show down a hand the vast majority of the time, so you must have good starting hand values, which usually means four connecting cards. You don't usually think about bluffing although occasions do come up when you can try it.

Peddling the Nuts. As T. J. puts it, "In all forms of Omaha people are usually peddling the nuts." That's true and in limit Omaha high, you get the nuts paid off more often than you do in pot-limit Omaha because it only costs your opponents an extra bet or two to call as opposed to their whole stack. This is why there is even less bluffing in limit high Omaha. "There's less bluffing in all types of Omaha than in any other poker games," T. J. adds. "When there's a gigantic pot in Omaha it's usually hand against hand, or set against set, or hand against a giant draw that might be the favorite."

Chasing. Because you usually are getting pot odds for your draws, it seems that a lot of players chase, especially at the lower limits. Just remember that when you chase, you still need to be drawing to the nuts. "And you should have more than just one draw — you should have a multiway draw," T. J. inserts. The point is that although you virtually always have proper pot odds, you still need to be drawing to the nuts or pretty close to it (or what you think is the nuts) most of the time. In that way, limit high Omaha is similar to the split version where the cardinal rule is that after the flop, you must be drawing to the nuts in one direction or the other in order to justify continuing with the hand.

A Tip from the Top
Always try to have a multiway draw.

T. J. explains the concept of having a *multiway* draw: "When I say a multiway draw, I mean that if you're drawing to a straight, you're usually not in there drawing at an open-end straight. It has to be some sort of a wraparound: top wrap, middle wrap or bottom wrap, like we explained in the pot-limit chapter. Obviously, the only time you're going to be playing a bottom wrap is when you're putting your opponent on a set and you know that if you make the low-end straight it will be good. The point is that you want to have more than one way to make your hand. An open-end straight draw is still just an open-end straight draw, no more."

Backdoor Hands. Of course, there are a lot more backdoor hands possible in Omaha. A lot of times, your backdoor out will come in. Your three-straights and three-flushes that go with your flop hand sometimes make the difference between calling and folding. I'll give you an example of hands that have a lot of backdoor value. Maybe you've flopped the top two pair with a straight draw and you also have two three-flushes. You're almost even money to pick up a flush draw on the turn card to go with your two pair. So, if you have two pair, a straight draw, and two three-flushes you have a pretty big hand, and you can prepare to put a lot of heat on the pot.

Even better is flopping a set and a couple of three-flushes. Often, when you make a backdoor flush, it doesn't need to be as strong as it would if it were your primary draw ... and that happens a lot. In the pot-limit version I know a top player who often will peel off a card just to pick up a draw, but that's usually not a good idea unless you have something else to go with it.

"If I have two three-flushes, they are *not* considered in my play" T. J. comments. If they come, they come, but I certainly don't consider them in the way I play the hand." Let me explain that you're not going with the hand on the basis of one or two three-flushes — you must have a two-pair hand or a set or a big wraparound. It's just that they add value to your hand. Also remember that if you backdoor a flush it usually won't be the nuts, but it still may be the best flush. It is less likely that you're going to run into a big flush (or any flush) when you backdoor one.

The Value of Playing Aggressively. "You can play more aggressively in the limit game than in the pot-limit version — and you *should* play more aggressively to maximize your win," T. J. adds. "In pot-limit you have to slow down a little because the pots get so big — you never have to worry about maximizing your bets because they're going to be maximized." In pot-limit you use the concept of implied odds. You know that the pot could build at a really rapid rate, so you're not as worried about maximizing your win as you are in limit.

"The biggest difference in pot-limit and limit high Omaha is that you shouldn't get broke on one hand in the limit game," T. J. reminds. "But a lot of times players will take chances in limit games. They'll call a couple of bets with big pairs and no connectors. If the big pair in their hand is higher than anything on the board, they will call a bet. Then they hope to hit their overpair on the turn and win the pot, which I think is a foolish play, but they do it."

STARTING HANDS

"In pot-limit and limit high Omaha," T. J. says, "the ranking of the hands is similar. A♠ A♣ J♠ 10♣ (any A-A-J-10 double-suited) is still the best starting hand in limit Omaha. In limit Omaha you play more hands and stand more one-bet raises than you do in pot-limit Omaha."

Players will play more hands in limit high Omaha because it's costing them only one or two bets whereas in pot-limit it could cost them their entire stacks. So, there are more players per hand in limit Omaha than in pot-limit. Usually, you'll get down to two players by fourth street in pot-limit Omaha, but in limit you might still have three, four or five players still in the hand.

Let's take another look at the starting hands for both versions of high Omaha:

Big Pairs with Connectors

The Big Rundowns

The Middle Rundowns

The Small Rundowns

Middle Pairs with Connectors

The main difference between pot-limit and limit high Omaha is not the hands that you start with, it's *how many* of them you play. In pot-limit, you can play one hand in an hour and make three or four times the chips you had when you started. In limit, you have to win a lot of hands to stay alive.

In limit high Omaha, you play the small rundowns more often and deeper into the hand. You also can play them up front — hands with four connectors or a pair with connectors such as 4-5-5-6, 4-5-6-7, 4-5-6-6, 5-6-7-7, or 6-7-8-8.

"Since there are more multiway pots in high Omaha, you can play more rundown hands" T. J. adds. "Playing marginal hands is just plain dumb in any poker game. And I repeat: Don't play hands with danglers."

"The worst dangler in the world is A-K-Q-7," T. J. asserts. "It's similar to razz when you start with a paint in the hole and two "perfects" (premium low cards) against a player with three perfects. Then you both catch perfect on fourth street and you have three perfects and your opponent has four — you're taking much the worse of it. If you have A-K-Q-2, at least you can make a straight with the deuce. It might not be the nuts, but you can make it.

"Of course, you're still in danger because of that dangler. Suppose you play A-K-Q-2 and the flop comes A-7-2. Now you have top and bottom pair, but what are you going to do with it? If somebody bets, you might be up against an A-7 or a set — you can get in a lot of trouble with that dangler."

It is common knowledge that hands like K♣ Q♣ 8♦ 7♦ are not good Omaha hands, but people sometimes play these types of hands, which is like having two hold'em hands. You want four cards that *interconnect* in some fashion, even if there is a gap. For example, J♣ 9♥ 9♣ 7♥ has gaps and isn't that strong a hand, but there are conditions under which I might play it — in an unraised pot, when there's multiway action and I'm on the button, or when I'm in the small blind for one-half a bet, that kind of thing. Being double-suited gives a little bit of added value to the hand, although I wouldn't be too excited about the flushes that I could make. At least, however, these are working cards — it's a hand that I think is substandard and weak but one that I might play in certain situations. But a hand like J♣ 9♣ 8♥ 3♥? No thank you. It's a piece of garbage ... and yet people play hands like that.

Although the standard starting hands in limit high Omaha are similar to pot-limit Omaha, the main difference is that you can go farther with the hands in limit than you can in pot-limit — and you can take more chances with them. Also, you may be more willing to come into the pot from first position with a hand like 4-5-6-7 in limit than in pot-limit (where they might pound you and you don't know how many other people will be coming into the pot).

Middle Connectors

The point is that I might be more willing to mix it up with middle or small connectors from early position in the limit game. I totally agree with T. J.'s philosophy that in pot-limit, you can play those cards for a small raise from late position because you're getting a big price and you have a chance to take somebody off who will gamble with you with just overpairs. But in limit games, there is even more reason to play them because there are so many more multiway pots in which you'll be getting the proper odds. You can play any four connecting cards if you can see the flop cheap. That is, any four connectors except for wheel cards (2-3-4-5 and so on). In pot-limit players force most of the players out of the pot with the big preflop betting, but in limit high Omaha that isn't the case.

We have said that you take more chances in limit Omaha. T. J. explains it this way: "Let's say that somebody raises — raised pots are very common in the limit game — and I have 3-4-5-6 in my hand. I'm probably going to play this hand in the limit game, whereas in pot-limit I'll play it only once in a while in a side game when I'm going to try to knock somebody off who has a lot of chips. In limit I'll play this hand because it costs only a certain amount of money every time. It doesn't cost you anymore to play that hand than it does to play a pair of aces. Then if you flop to it, you'll take somebody off who is playing a big pair.

"In limit high Omaha, if a player has two aces and the flop comes 9-7-2 (a hand where somebody could have a wraparound), he's liable to lead at the pot. If you had 10-8-7-6 in your hand, he's in trouble. That's why you play these types of hands once in a while in limit while you can't always play them in pot-limit."

T. J. continues with another valuable point: "My theory is that you should always have suits in Omaha, even in limit games. But you don't necessarily want to have 3-4-5-6 with suits because if two flush cards come out on the flop, what are you going to do? Try to draw to a six-high flush? You're only hoping to make a straight with a low rundown hand like that."

He's right. Also, any four connecting cards are usually worth calling a raise. Again, in limit you can't get broke to the hand whereas in pot-limit you can get broke to it. In any form of big-bet poker, you can often distort the pot odds to make the drawing price unprofitable, whereas in limit games you can't. These wraparound straight draws against overpairs are huge favorites with two cards to come and yet, players still get married to their aces in Omaha, just like they do in most other games.

"If you're watching your players and learning how they're playing and seeing what they're showing down, the kinds of hands they play," T. J. reminds us, "you'll know what kinds of hands they raise with. If you know that a guy only raises with aces or aces suited or kings, you're going to play the small rundowns such as 4-5-6-7 against him because you're trying to take him off the aces. If you don't flop to it, the hand's easy to get away from."

Raising Hands

Raising hands include a big rundown such as A-K-Q-J double-suited (or at least single-suited), or a big pair with connectors such as K-J-K-10 with at least one suit. You also can raise with rundowns such as a J-10-9-8 or a Q-J-10-9 *when* you are in late position and are the *first* one in the pot.

When you have big pot odds in limit high Omaha, your primary reason to raise before the flop is to build the pot. You want people who are willing to gamble to pay a price even though, many times, you may have to abandon your big cards on the flop. Also, you can raise from any position to build a pot because you can't get broke by raising.

Your raise might force some of the marginal holdings out, of course, but if it's a wide open game and they'll gamble with you, you want to make them take the worst of it while you still have the best of it (before the flop). You want to make your opponents who are drawing to worse starting hands put in their money up front. It is always correct to raise to try to build the pot under these game conditions.

PLAYING THE FLOP

If you don't hit anything on the flop, obviously you fold the hand. The kinds of draws you want to flop are those in which you have *more than one draw* to a hand that you think will win the pot. When I have a hand that gets there on the flop, the only question in my mind is, "How do I maximize my profit?" I don't want to give a free card if a free card is likely to beat me.

If I'm first to act, the question is, "Do I think my opponent(s) will bet if I check?" When a scary flop or a scare card comes in Omaha, a lot of players may not want to bet but they will call you if you bet. You have to sense this type of thing. So, I will play my hand in a straightforward fashion most of the time. I'm not going to try the fancy check-raise nearly as often as I might in hold'em, I'm just going to fire away at my opponent(s).

If I think that I have the best hand, especially if I think that my opponent(s) has a set and will probably try to draw to fill up, why give him a free card? Suppose I am on a flush draw, for example, and the obvious flush card comes on the turn. If I check, he's most likely also going to check if he has a set, so it makes no sense to check to him.

Also, you usually have more than one opponent in limit high Omaha. If several of the players are even halfway decent, they will be afraid of that flush card, so you have to bet your own hand. You have do your own dirty work — you have to bet your hand rather than hope that someone else will bet it for you. I don't ask others to do something that I am not prepared to do myself (unless it's housework ... then I'm willing to pay somebody to do that!).

Giving Free Cards

T. J. has said that the only hands you can give free cards with are the nuts where you can't be drawn out on. We were talking about flopping quads and he said that he would go right ahead and bet them because people are usually going to call him anyway. Whether I would slowplay the quads depends on the texture of the flop. I might tend less to slowplay them if, for example, I have a pair of queens and the flop comes K-Q-Q. I'm more likely to bet the queens in that situation, especially if the king is suited to one of the queens. Then at least people would have a reason to play with me because they might have possibilities for drawing to flushes or straights — drawing dead, of course, unless they have a royal flush draw. But if it comes a rainbow flop with three mixed suits and a non-connecting card (Q-Q-4, for example) then I think you almost have to check at least once to allow someone to try to catch something.

Another factor is how likely your opponents are to draw dead. Some players who are really nutted up are not going to draw to a nut flush when the board has already paired. In this case, you have to check at least once to create some doubt in their mind that you have a big hand. But if you're playing with people who will gamble, which is what you want, then go ahead and fire away. One nice thing about betting the nuts in any form of poker, Omaha in particular, is that when you fire right out with it very seldom do they give you credit for the nuts. Not only the texture of the flop, but the texture of the game dictates a lot of your betting strategy.

Free Cards in Tournaments. In tournaments it's different. "People who give free cards in tournaments are just asking to get slaughtered," is the way T. J. puts it. That is correct, so the only hands worth checking in a tournament are the mortal nuts or close to it. But if your opponents are will-

127

ing to mix it up, you don't even check the absolute nuts if it looks like there are drawing possibilities.

T. J. adds: "One other hand that I think you can give free cards is a straight that can't be improved in pot-limit Omaha. If you get action in front of you, are you going to raise with this hand right now? There might be two to a suit or a set out there. I don't think of just calling in this situation as slow-playing the hand ... you do it because you want to see what comes on fourth street before you get further involved. I'm just playing the hand *slow,* I'm not slowplaying the hand."

I see the point he is making, and we can relate it to limit high Omaha. Sometimes, for example, you and an opponent each have the opportunity to draw out on the other. Someone could have a set to go with his nut straight, or maybe you have a flush draw to go with your nut straight. (This type of thing comes up frequently in pot-limit. People have thrown away what they knew was the nuts at the moment because they knew their opponent also had the nuts plus a freeroll against them.) But in limit high Omaha if I have the nuts at the moment, or if I think it might be vulnerable, even if I suspect that someone else also has the nuts I still may put in a raise to try to narrow the field.

Now, if my opponent plays back at me and he has the nuts and I have the nuts, and if he's a reasonable player, I'll just call. This happens most often when you both have the nut straight with no other draws to improve the hand. When that occurs, I have to slow down and, if my opponent is a reasonable player, ask myself, "What is he raising me with? I've tested him once and narrowed the field."

If I'm in front position and have the nut straight, it might go this way: I bet it, a guy raises after me, and I reraise to narrow the field of players yet to act between me and him ... as long as I have the nuts, that is. Or if I think that my opponent has the nuts and so do I — but I also have a freeroll against him — I will most likely reraise. If he's flopped the nuts, he can't go anywhere in the limit version. Although great pot-limit players will occasionally lay down the nuts on the flop, there is less reason to do this in limit Omaha because you can't get broke to the hand.

In all forms of Omaha the nut hand is out there more often than in other poker games. This almost always is true where straights are concerned — and the nut straight can easily be out in more than one hand.

T. J. gives another example of slowplaying, this time in a tournament situation: "Suppose you have an A-K in hold'em and the flop comes A-A-10. You check and it's checked all around. Then on the turn comes a jack. Now what are you going to do with this hand? Someone may have a K-Q in his hand and make the nut straight on the turn because you gave him a free card on the flop."

That's true. Suppose someone has a small pocket pair — sixes, for example. A six comes on the turn, which looks like an innocent card. Because you gave that little pair a free card on the flop, he now has a full house and you're still drawing. This is even more likely to happen in Omaha where people have four cards to start with and usually have more starting pairs. So if you have flopped the nuts or close to it, you don't want to give free cards that possibly will allow your opponents to beat you. You're in a spot in which your opponent may be able to beat you, but he can't call a bet anyway *unless* he *can* beat you. So it makes no sense to give him a free card because he can't give you any action anyway unless he has caught a magic card that beats you.

A Tip from the Top
You always want to make the play that will maximize your profit.

You want to make the play that you believe will maximize the money that you can make on that hand. For that reason, you can play more aggressively in limit high Omaha because very often it is that aggressiveness that will maximize your profit.

Actually, in limit high Omaha there usually is less reason to disguise the strength of your hand. People will find excuses to get in the pot anyway, so what you want to do is make people pay to draw against you as long as you think you have the best of it. Or if you have such a big draw yourself that you're a favorite over even a set, you should charge forward.

Decision Hands

"You're going to run into a lot of the 'decision' hands that we discussed in the general principles section of this book," T. J. wisely adds. "Usually, these decision hands in limit high Omaha are the middle rundown hands. You have to decide whether you want to get involved with them or not, which partly depends on how well you know your opponents. You've seen how the players are playing. If they're playing high cards all the time and they're playing solid, you might take them off with a middle rundown hand. You have to decide whether you want to try that."

Another time that you run into a decision situation is using your ability to determine when your king or queen-high flush is good enough to win. The good players can tell from the way the betting is going, and who's doing the betting, when it's OK to draw to these hands.

PLAYING THE TURN

Suppose you called the flop with a flush draw. On the turn you miss it. Now what do you do? If you can get a free card, that's great, but even if you don't, you still can call a single bet if you are drawing to the nuts. What I don't want to have happen is to get caught in the middle between two people who are at war with each other. If that is likely to happen, or if I call and then the war breaks out behind me with one card to come, I must abandon the hand unless I have other possibilities. If I have other draws to go with my flush draw that could also prove to be the best hand, then a lot of times I'll take the heat and continue with the hand.

Other types of draws might be a big wraparound or a two-pair hand *if* my two pair are the top two pair. If I think that I'm up against a set and I have top two pair, I might call hoping that I can pair up one of my top two cards. For example, let's say that I have:

The flop comes:

I know that there's a straight out there, but I have two pair and the nut flush draw. If two people start going to town or if a super tight player puts in a raise, I know that I'm up against a made straight. But I have top two pair, the nut flush draw, and the ace with connectors so that I could catch a 10 to make the big straight and either win the pot or split it. If a nondescript card comes on the turn (I don't catch any of my outs), even if there's a raising war, I'm still covered and will draw with one card to come. Of course, I would give it up if the board paired on the turn and it wasn't my pair (the board paired the jacks).

If all I have is the flush draw, my play would be different. This time, suppose my cards are:

A blank comes on the turn, so that the board reads:

Two people in front of me start going to war when the blank hits. In this case, I would abandon ship because all I have is the flush draw.

However, if it costs me only one bet, I would call to see the river card because the pot usually is giving me a big enough price (approximately 4-to-1 with one card to come) to justify making the call *for a single bet*. For a single bet — that's the key. If someone bets, I call, someone behind me raises and then the original bettor reraises, I would give up. But suppose there's a bet, I call, someone raises, and the original bettor just calls? Then I also would call. In other words, I might call a single bet twice but not a double bet once.

This example applies strictly to those occasions when you have only *one* way to make the hand and are not involved in a raising war. Also, you have some extra implied odds. Although you're a 4-to-1 dog, the pot usually is so big that even if the flush card comes, people will grumble about how lucky you are but they often will reluctantly pay you off anyway. Or sometimes they also may have made a flush and feel forced to pay it off on the end. And it gets even sweeter when an opponent with a flush draw that he thought was the best one bets into you and you raise him. If he's a bad enough player to bet less than the nut flush under these conditions, chances are that he's a bad enough player to pay off the raise, too!

When a Scare Card Comes on the Turn

Suppose I have drawn to my hand on the flop and the turn card is a very scary card so that I am no longer sure that I'm drawing to the nuts — there's a lot of doubt in my mind. For example, suppose I have:

The flop comes with the Q♦ J♣ 4♠. I've flopped top two pair and I have a straight draw, but I'm only happy hitting an eight, a queen or a jack. I'm not happy hitting an ace, king, ten or nine.

Now suppose a straight card comes on the turn, either a king or a nine that can make a bigger straight than what I'm drawing to. Take a look at the flop and turn cards:

I am forced to check the hand because there's a good chance that I'm already beat. I'm reduced to possibly a six-out full house. Therefore, what was a reasonably strong hand that I might have heavily gambled with on the flop becomes very vulnerable on the turn. Plus, with two suited cards out there if the other suited card comes and I don't have a flush draw, then what do I have? Zilch!

Or even worse, suppose I flopped a straight. I may have a K-Q-Q-J, a decent starting hand. The flop comes 10-9-8 with two of a suit. I flopped the nut straight and can even draw to a slightly higher straight if a jack comes. Then boom! The third suited card hits. What do I have now?! I'm done with it — I have to check-pass a hand that I was willing to push to the hilt on the flop.

Omaha high can be brutal! It's a cold, cruel world and it's a cold, cruel game. (But it's not as cold and cruel as Omaha split, which is even more aggravating!)

Tom McEvoy, 1992 limit high Omaha World Champion

PLAYING AT THE RIVER

The river pretty much takes care of itself in limit high Omaha. There's a lot of drawing going on in this game, which means that the river card can drastically influence the results. You might have had the nuts all along and it turns into a pile of manure at the end. The board pairs or the flush card gets there when you've had the nuts all the way. Or you draw to the nuts on the flop, make it on fourth street, and then someone makes the bigger nuts at the river.

This happens a lot. And this is why Omaha players gnash their teeth a lot and have little stubs for eye teeth instead of full-sized dentals. It's similar to Omaha high-low where you've flopped the wheel with your A-2 and a deuce comes on the turn. Now there's so many people with six-high straights that instead of scooping the pot you'll get three-quartered or worse. I once made a wheel without the board getting paired, got counterfeited at the end, and wound up with one-sixth of the pot. Three people made six-high straights *and* the wheel! Dana says I'm a cry baby. OK, no more sniveling for me — you have to be mentally tough to play Omaha high-low! And mental toughness is a good trait to have in limit high Omaha, too.

Now suppose that on the river you miss your hand and it looks like everybody else has missed, too. You're in an end position and everybody checks to you. You're sitting there with two pair. Do you bet? If I have two pair that could win a showdown. I am *less* likely to bet if I think that I won't get called *unless* I'm beat. But if I think that I have the best hand and might get a call, then I may very well bet.

A Steal Situation. But what if I think that everybody was on a draw and they have all missed on the end — and so have I? Occasionally, this is an opportunity to steal a pot. I'm not going to try to steal against four or five people, which is what I call Omaha suicide. But suppose a backdoor flush card hits and I'm last to act. I have one or two opponents and they both check. I was drawing to something else, but now they're afraid of this scare card that has come out there. I have nothing ... this may be an opportunity to try to steal.

I don't try to steal very often. I have to be in exactly the right situation against people who are capable of laying down a hand and are a little bit on the tight side ... or if they're timid and freeze up every time a scare card hits. In this type of situation, I may very well bet with nothing on the end. If you try it yourself and get called in a similar situation, you might as well just turn your cards face down and throw them in the muck. Someone with some little teeny flush or a low two-pair was too timid to bet it, but he was brave enough to call you. You have to sort of know these things about your opponents.

You don't try to bluff people who are timid but will check-call. You bluff people who will lay down a hand when they think that you might have made something. And you wouldn't even think of trying to bluff three or more players. Most of the time, I don't think about bluffing at all. But occasionally, you can make this type of positional play at the pot against one or two opponents who you think are capable of laying down some hands that you couldn't beat in a legitimate showdown.

If I think that a bet has a negative expectation — that I probably will get called only if I am beat — I wouldn't bet, I would just show it down. And that happens a lot. Negative expectation bets come up more frequently in Omaha than they do in hold'em, for example. When the only way that you can get called is if you're beat, it makes no sense to bet. If you have a medium two-pair that may or may not be good because your opponents were on draws that didn't materialize, they can't call you, can they? But if one of them has a bigger two-pair or a small set, he probably will check-call you. So you have to decide whether a bet on the end has a negative expectation.

Some Tips on Tournament Play

In limit high Omaha tournaments you actually have to be a little bit more conservative than you are in ring games to preserve your chips ... unless you have a ton of chips. If I have a bunch of chips, I am more likely to be willing to mix it up with hands that are reasonable, though not great, holdings. This is when I'll take the four small connectors like 7-6-5-4 and raise from up front. I have a lot of chips, everybody's shortstacked trying to hang on and they don't want to mess with me.

When You Have a Big Stack. When I have a big stack I'll pound away with hands that are less than premium but still have potential. And if I miss the flop, guess what? I'll just dump the hand. But I'll put some heat on them before the flop. And if I'm heads-up, I might put in one bet on the end even if I miss because a lot of times they're trying to preserve their chips in an effort to hang on to get to the pay table.

I admit it: I love being a bully. Unfortunately, the opportunities don't come up that often because it's difficult to accumulate a lot of chips. Dana says that all accountants love to be bullies because they didn't have a chance to do that in their former 9-to-5 jobs. That's correct. When I was in that 9-to-5 accounting job back in the '70s, I was the one who always got sand kicked in my face. Today in the poker world, I get a chance to kick a little sand of my own.

The point is that when you have chips, you can open it up a little bit, but you don't open it up with trash hands. Sometimes, however, you *can* do it with anything. I'll give you an example of the one time when it didn't matter what my hole cards were. In the 1984 World Series of Poker, the first time a pot-limit hold'em event was staged, we were down to ten players. I had by far the biggest stack and there were several people just barely hanging on trying to make the last table because it only paid nine places, so I started just raising and playing every single hand.

More recently, a player from Michigan who has never before or since won a poker tournament did the same thing in the limit high Omaha tournament at the WSOP. He had accumulated a massive amount of chips so he simply began raising and playing every single hand. He couldn't have had a hand every single time, but it seems that when anybody took a stand he would show them a hand. He was super loose, super aggressive, and played *every* hand. I've never seen anything like it: He bulldozed the entire table. This recreational player won a WSOP title just by using these aggressive tactics.

In the opening stages of the tournament, however, hand value is where it's at ... until you can reach the point where you can be the bully. When you can't be the bully, you have to show down a hand most of the time. This is a show-down-a-hand game.

Playing a Dangler. There is one situation in a tournament when I might play a dreaded dangler hand — specifically when I am in the small blind. I really don't like danglers, but if I have three *very* decent cards and it's only going to cost me one-half a bet, this is the one time when I am more willing to call with a dangler hand. In particular, if I have at least one nut-flush draw, one ace working, I will make the call. I also feel the same way about the big blind if all I have to call is a single raise — it will cost me only one more bet when somebody raises, especially if there are several people already in the pot.

I don't have a very good hand. Suppose I have:

The ace is suited, plus I have some slight straight chances and a minimal wheel chance. This is not a great hand, but under these conditions I would call a single raise with this hand. I'm also prepared to play with extreme caution on the flop if it doesn't come just right for me. One nut flush and a couple of marginal straight possibilities are my minimum requirements for a dangler hand in these circumstances.

The 1992 Championship Game. When I won the limit Omaha title in 1992 against Berry Johnston, a key hand came up while we were still in a ring-game situation that shocked me. There were some pretty good players at the last table — Frank Henderson, Brent Carter, Mel Judah, An Tran, Jim Boyd, Berry Johnston and me. And that's why I treasure my victory so highly. (Mr. Cloutier has now caught me in the bracelet race with four each, and that greatly saddens me. What's more, he passed me on the money list this year too.)

I was in the big blind in an unraised pot with a real junky looking hand, something like 6♥ 7♥ 8♣ Q♠. I flopped a straight flush! Mel Judah flopped the ace-high flush. He was still trying to survive at that point. Judah had been playing ultra solid. I decided to lead with the straight flush rather than slowplay because I figured that if someone had the nut flush (the ace high), I might get some action. So, I just fired at the pot. Judah called and everybody else passed. The turn card came a blank. I bet again. He just called. The board didn't pair on the river. I bet again. Again he just called.

140

When he turned over the ace-high flush, I said to him "How the hell could you just call with the nut flush?!" He answered, "I smelled a rat. What else could you have?" This shows how smart he is. Almost anybody else would've raised with that nut flush.

"I disagree that almost anybody else would've raised that pot," T. J. argues. "If you have the nut flush and a man has led at you three times, what hand are you going to give him if there's a straight flush possibility out there?"

"Would you have played it differently?" Dana asked T. J.

"I don't even know if I would have made the last call," he answered. "It's hard to lay the nut flush down, but here you've made it and the other man's a player and he's doing the leading ... what the hell can he have but the straight flush? A player the caliber of Tom ... what's he going do? Lead out with the second or third-nut flush three times in a row?!"

"Well," I answered, "when Judah called me that last time, he did squirm in his chair a little bit! But he lost the absolute minimum on the hand and I was impressed with his play. The average player would've raised with that hand and lost a lot more to it."

I can see T. J.'s point, though — there were some very skilled players at that final table. I don't know how the others would've played it, I only know how Mel played it. Of course, Mel won a bracelet in 1998 in seven-card stud and took third place in the championship event in 1997 against Stu Ungar and John Stzremp.

Another Championship Story. T. J. tells this story about winning his first World Series bracelet: "My first bracelet at the WSOP was in limit high Omaha, but I can't remember a single person who was at the final table! I just remember that it was the first time I'd ever played limit high Omaha in my entire life. And then my wife Joy and I went to Lafayette for the Cajun Cup and I won the same event there, too. I won those two tournaments back to back.

"Carl McKelvey and I played four and a half hours heads-up for the championship. That was a battle. I guess the only reason that I won is because I was really aggressive. Anything that came out there, I was representing. And I wouldn't slow down ... I was firing all the way. You know, if a guy's firing all the way, sometimes it's hard to call without having the nuts."

That's what happened when I played Berry Johnston heads-up in 1992 at the final table. He was definitely playing a little more conservatively than I was, and he had the chip lead most of the way. He made a couple of laydowns in situations where, if he'd called, I don't know if I could've taken the pot. But I represented what was out there and I figured that he was drawing to something — maybe he had two pair and a draw, but a flush card hit, and so I bet it. A lot of times when you have the ace to the suit that's showing on the board, you can represent the nut flush because you know that no one else has it.

"Yes, but you can only do that a few times," T. J. reminds us. "Any player will pick you right off if you try it too often." In limit high Omaha it's a little bit more risky because it only costs a single bet for an opponent to call.

The Big Comeback. But back to the WSOP: Berry made laydowns in a couple of hands that allowed me to survive. That tournament also was the biggest comeback I've ever had at a World Series event. At one point, Berry had 90 percent of the chips. That's one reason I'm so proud of that victory. Berry himself has done the same thing ... has come back from a seemingly hopeless deficit to win. The point is that anyone — including you — can come back from near disaster and make a fine finish in a tournament. It just takes determination, timing, and a tiny bit of luck.

Playing Against Super Aggressive Opponents.

"Speaking of being aggressive in tournaments," T. J. adds, "a man who I know to be a really good tournament player told me that he can't figure out how to play against the Kamikaze pilots, guys that you know are going to represent everything on the flop every time. He says he doesn't know whether to play tight or loose or just real solid.

"The answer is that you just play *your* game. Let them play the way they want to play, but you always play your game. If your game is good enough, you're going to get the money. There isn't a poker player alive who doesn't lose, but in the long run the best players end up with the money.

"You see, you can never judge poker by one game or one evening's play. A poker player judges himself by what he does for the year. One guy told me that he judges himself by the hides on his wall — if he has all the hides and you don't have any, he must be the best player." ♣

Chapter 5

OMAHA PRACTICE HANDS

by T. J. Cloutier
Commentary by Tom McEvoy

Practice Hand One

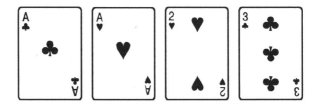

Omaha High-Low

This is the optimum hand you can be dealt in high-low. I usually would raise or reraise with this hand before the flop from a late position, even if the aces are single-suited or unsuited. If you flop two little cards, a flush draw or top set, you have a huge hand. When you catch a good flop, play this hand strong. Why not? This is a limit game, so it can't cost you that much if you're on a draw and miss it. If they don't bet, *you* bet.

But if you don't flop to it, get rid of the hand if there is any action in front of you. All you have then is two aces, so what's the point in continuing? You couldn't ask for a better starting hand, but why lose money to it if the flop comes with a Q-J-10 or 10-9-8 or something like that? If it comes with two high cards and one low card, you would need to catch runner-runner little cards to make the low. Against any action somebody else already has a high hand with that type of board, so your aces are no longer a factor.

144

A big mistake that some high-low players make when they start with a strong hand like this is catching only one little card on the flop with no other outs and then drawing for a second low card on the turn. Sure enough, they catch that little card and then get hooked into drawing for a third one. Almost invariably the board rags off on the end or comes with a third high-straight card and the chasers are out of the race.

Pot-Limit Omaha

You slow down with this hand in pot-limit. The only situation in which I would play it strong is when I could reraise with the aces where the raise is coming in to me, to try to isolate with one or two other players. Remember that you can *reraise* with aces, but you don't raise with them.

You're in danger with this hand on the flop if it comes something like 4-5-9 and none of your suit because someone else might have the 8-7-6-5 and be drawing to a higher straight when the best straight you could make is a six-high. Although this is the best starting hand in high-low, you have to be careful with it in pot-limit.

Interestingly, you can be aggressive in the high-low game with the best pot-limit starting hand — the A-J-A-10 double-suited — but in pot-limit you cannot be aggressive with the best high-low starting hand. If you have A-A-J-10 in high-low and no low comes on the flop, you have the opportunity to scoop the pot. But with A-A-2-3 in pot-limit, the number of good hands that will hold up are far more limited, so you play it softer than you would in the high-low game.

Limit High Omaha

In limit high Omaha, I definitely would put in one pre-flop raise with the two aces if they are single-suited or double-suited. It's always nice to have at least one suit and you're in hog heaven when you have two — but if the aces are un-suited, I would not raise before the flop.

Practice Hand 2

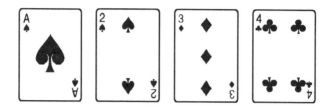

Omaha High-Low

A-2-3-4 is the second best Omaha high-low hand you can get. You'd like to have it suited to the ace, but even if it isn't suited, this is still a very strong hand. You can stand as many raises as you have to with this one.

Just remember that when you start off, you're only playing a low hand if the ace isn't suited. Obviously, you can make a wheel or a low straight that will scoop the pot, but keep in mind that you're usually playing for only the low end of the pot. For that reason, you don't want to make an initial raise with A-2-3-4 unsuited.

You can play back with it if you want to, but I would not make the first raise with this hand — let somebody else do the raising. A lot of times, you will tip off the strength of your hand when you put in that first raise. Why would you want to tip off your strength on a hand that you might get paid big money on later?

If the ace is suited, this is a raising hand. Now you're thinking that you might be able to scoop the pot. The whole idea of Omaha high-low is to scoop the pot — the players who scoop the most pots are the ones who win the tournaments or the money in the side games.

Of course, you have a chance of scooping the pot even if the ace isn't suited, but you need a big, big flop to do it. Naturally, if the flop comes A-A-2, A-A-3 or A-A-4, you have a huge hand. In fact, the flop doesn't even need to come with two aces for you to have a big hand. If it comes with an A-2, A-3 or A-4, you have two pair, plus you're still drawing at the nut low. The flop can counterfeit two of your cards and you'll still have the boss low drawing hand.

Pot-Limit Omaha and Limit Omaha High

This is not a playable hand in the high games unless you happen to get stiffed in with it and catch the absolute optimum flop to it. Otherwise, do not play it. Sure, you have a suited ace, but other than that this is a nothing-hand.

Obviously, the K-K-Q-J double-suited is a powerful hand. Just remember that it's powerful as long as an ace doesn't hit the board. Once an ace hits the board and you haven't flopped any of your cards, you're in deep trouble. Suppose the flops comes:

A ten will make a straight for you, but that one lone ace on the board has you beaten right now, so just get rid of it. The hand looks powerful as hell to start with, but you still need the right flop to it.

Notice that the board has come with three suits and two of them are yours, one heart and one club. Even though the ace is out there, a lot of people will play the hand anyway when one card in each of their suits is also on the board, rationalizing "I have two backdoor flushes." This is not a good move. As I said earlier, fourth street can kill you because it almost always seems to give you another flush card. So now you've picked up the flush draw on the turn, thinking "Well, I can make the big flush at the river and win this pot." Almost invariably, you aren't going to make it. When you're hoping for runner-runner, the odds against you are just too high to go for it. I don't care if you have two three-flushes, it isn't worth playing. Now suppose the board comes 2-7-10. You check it. You hope that you get a showdown pot, or that you pick up a king or something on fourth street. I wouldn't get involved with the hand just because I have a big overpair. If somebody bets, I'd get rid of it. If you haven't raised with this hand going in, what's the point? You don't have that much invested.

This is a raising hand in pot-limit Omaha — but if you get reraised you have a piece of cheese. In limit high Omaha, you play the hand more; that is, you might play that top pair. But in pot-limit Omaha, if an ace hits the board or if there's any action on the flop, two kings is nothing.

Now suppose you're in an Omaha high-low game and the flop comes 8-8-6. I've seen people call a bet on the flop with a big overpair against that type of flop, but I wouldn't do it. Why waste the money? You're calling with an overpair trying to catch a two-outer twice — with two cards to come you have a four-outer. And with two low cards on the flop, you're most likely up against two (or more) low draws so that even if you catch a king, you will have to split the pot if another (unpaired) low card also comes.

The principles of poker apply to all games. If you put a guy on a stone bluff in the high games and you're trying to pick him off, that's different. But this is where intuition and watching the play comes in — knowing who will try to run a bluff and who won't. Most of the time you'd better go south for the winter when you have K-K-Q-J and the board shows a low pair like 8-8-6. That's all there is to it.

Omaha is a game of peddling the nuts — people do it a lot more in the Omaha games than they ever do in hold'em. If you're sitting there with a king-high flush and a guy is leading at you putting money in the pot, your king-high flush suddenly is like a three-high flush (and I've never seen one of those!). Ninety percent of the time he has the ace-high flush. Once in a while, somebody might play that "lone ace" bluff at a flush when he has the ace of the suit, but not very often.

If the flop comes with three clubs, there are some players who think they have a real hand with a ten-high flush. They think they have the stone nuts and you can't get them out of the pot for all the tea in China. Naturally, you want to play against these kinds of guys. But real players are going to show you a hand. When the money gets there, they're *there*.

We're describing optimum Omaha situations in this book, but there are situations that arise in every poker game in which you have to go away from what you *should* do and play what you *know* — play the player, just like you do in hold'em. Who's playing the hand against you? How do they play? Are they good players? Are they weak players? But always remember that anybody, weak or strong, can be dealt a good hand. The real skill comes down to whether your instincts are right or wrong in these types of situations.

Practice Hand 4

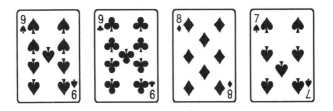

Omaha High-Low

Without exception, I will never play a 9-9-8-7 in Omaha high-low. The only time you would play it in this game is when you're stiffed in — you're in the big blind or it only costs you one more chip in the little blind. In Omaha high-low, play big cards and play little cards. And when I say "little" cards, I don't mean that you should get stuck in there with a damned hand like 3-4-5-6. All those hands do is chew up your money.

Pot-Limit and Limit High Omaha

In limit high Omaha, I'll play the 9-9-8-7 but I don't want to stand a raise with it — I don't want to put myself in a jammed pot with it. I just come in for the original bet and if I get raised I'll release it *unless* there is three or four-way action. In that case, you're getting good enough odds to play this hand. If you put this guy on aces and that guy on kings — the optimum situation is where you're good enough at the game that you can put them *both* on aces — then you're playing live cards, which is the way to bust those guys.

Now suppose the flop comes:

Here's a flop where you have made a straight but don't have any opportunity to improve. If there's more than one player giving action in this hand, you're supposed to throw it away. This flop cancels out any idea you might've had about making a set, and there's a flush draw out there. If you have to go against two other hands, you're actually a dog ... even though you flopped the nuts. Remember, pot-limit Omaha is the only game in which you can flop the nuts and throw it away and never lose any money.

In limit high Omaha if you're raised on the flop, you're going to play the hand until something hits the board that can beat you and then you release it. But if you flop the nuts in pot-limit Omaha and you bet and you get raised in a couple of spots — or if one guy bets, another guy calls, you raise and they both call — you're a dog.

Now let's suppose the flop comes 9-9-5. In pot-limit, you can check your quads but in limit games I would always lead at the pot and hope that someone plays back at me. There's nothing wrong with leading with huge hands, especially in limit poker, hoping that you get played with. In pot-limit, I would let my opponent take the lead on the flop and just flat call, so that I could punish him on fourth and fifth streets.

Practice Hand 5

A-A with any two face cards double-suited or with just one suit is a big, big hand in all forms of Omaha. As far as I'm concerned, this is the best hand you can have in pot-limit Omaha. This is the one hand where I'll go away from my rule of never being the original raiser with aces before the flop. With this hand I will raise before the flop from any position, in all three types of Omaha games.

If you have A-A-J-10 the board might even come with 10-10-4 giving you top set with top kicker and overcards. Even if someone has two fours in the hole, for example, you still have cards that you can hit that will take him off the hand ... the jack, the aces. So, you still have a strong hand.

In Omaha high-low the low might not come, you know, and you have all sorts of nut-straight and nut-flush possibilities, plus you have the pair of aces. If the flop comes with all low cards, you can get away from it — it has only cost you a bet and a raise.

In pot-limit or limit Omaha, if you get any kind of connected flop to this hand, you're going with it because it's such a big hand. Suppose the flop comes K-Q-8 with two cards in one of your suits. You have a monster! You have an overpair, a double middle-buster and a flush draw. You have nine flush cards and six straight cards, plus the two aces. You have 17 times two, which is 34 pure wins. You *have* to play those kinds of hands!

In most of the straights that you want to draw to in high Omaha, there should be three or four cards that can make a straight for you. If you play an open-ender in hold'em, you just have eight wins, but in Omaha you want to have more wins than that. The key in high Omaha is having a big hand and drawing at an even bigger hand so that you can cut off other players. If they make their hand, you're there too. You have to think about all these things as you're playing.

Now let's look at another flop:

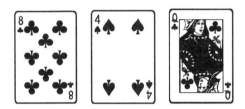

This may not look like that great a flop at first glance, but do you see what you have here? A single middle buster, an overpair and a flush draw — a lot of ways to make the hand.

Now let's take a look at what might happen in Omaha when the board pairs and you have an overpair. Suppose the eight pairs on the turn:

Against any action, you have to give it up. But what if there is no action? If someone checks to you, you also check. Sometimes you can win in high Omaha with aces-up when the board pairs like this, but why would you lead at it with a bet on the end? All somebody needs to beat you is one little eight. In pot-limit it's not just wasting a bet, it's more than that. It's like betting a four-flush with one card to come — you make the bet and somebody comes over the top of you, and then you have to dump the hand. When the board pairs, all you have with those aces-up is a *draw* with one card to come. There's a big difference. Once that board pairs, it's checkdown time.

If somebody leads at it big, you act according to who the player is and what you've been watching him do on the end. Suppose he checks after the boards pairs the eight. Then a blank comes on the river and he leads at it. Now you're put to the decision. What you decide to do depends on what you know about this player — how good a player he is. Would he bluff at this pot? Could he have two jacks in the hole, or maybe a lone queen? What could you beat with aces up? Remember, don't try to *invent* a hand that you can beat — don't call unless you think you can win the pot with the hand you have.

Practice Hand 6

Omaha High-Low

The only way you're thinking about playing this hand in Omaha high-low is playing the aces or the two nut-flush draws for high because the 5-6 is a tough low. But in the broad sense of the game, sometimes the A-5 or the A-6 will work for low, usually when you're heads-up and your opponent happens to be playing high, too.

In other words, you don't enter the hand thinking that the 5-6 is going to play for a low hand. You're thinking of making the high flush or three aces — or possibly catching a 3-4, which would be a fabulous flop to this hand because then you would have the straight draw and the nut-low draw. Suppose the flop comes with two little cards:

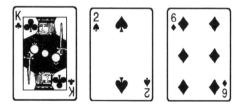

Here you have flopped a draw to the second nut low and an overpair. Against this flop, I'm through with the hand. I've seen some players take a card off, mainly because of the overpair but also because they have two backdoor flush possibilities with the K♣ and the 2♠ on the flop. But I don't give as much credit to backdoor flushes as some people do. To me, that backdoor possibility is not a factor that I consider in the play of the hand, it's just an added element that might come to pass. My play of a hand is based on its merit at the time. Now suppose the flop comes:

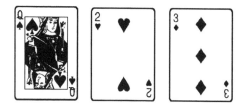

I'm going to play this hand on the flop. There is always the chance that the deuce or trey has counterfeited somebody else's hand for low, whereas with the K-2-6 flop it doesn't appear that anybody's low has been completely counterfeited. Suppose you draw and out pops the A♦ on the turn:

There's a strong possibility that someone has the 4-5 and has made a wheel, so what do you do now? You never lead at the pot, you trail with it ...that's all you can do.

But if there is a bet and raise before the action gets to me, I'm throwing this hand away. Somebody already has the wheel so what am I doing here? Drawing to catch a four to tie for the low? Or pair the board to win one-half of the pot?

Now let's say that the flop comes:

You have the second-nut low draw and the nut flush draw. You play the hand on the flop, of course. Again the A♦ comes on the turn:

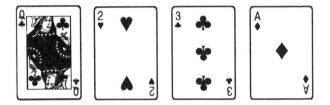

Now how do you play the hand? You go for it. In this scenario, you have a playing hand with a lot of outs.

Limit High Omaha

This is a very good hand in limit high Omaha — it is a raising hand when it's double-suited or single-suited. But without a suit, I don't think this is a raising hand in any variety of Omaha. In pot-limit, this is a *reraising* hand *only* if you think that you can isolate the field to one other player. You don't want to go against three or four players without being double suited, whereas in Omaha high-low you'll see the flop with A-A-5-6 whether it's suited or not.

Pot-Limit Omaha

A-A-5-6 double-suited is a good hand in pot-limit and limit high Omaha. In these two games you're again looking for nut flushes or three aces — or a 2-3-4 flop would be fabulous. And a 3-4-7 would be a great flop to this hand because you would have the nuts. Even if an eight hit the board on the turn, you still would have the nuts.

In the long run, this is a good hand when you get certain flops to it, but you don't want to see a middle flop with this hand. For example, if an 8-7-2 came on the flop, I'm a goner. In this scenario, the optimum card to catch is a four but if a nine, ten or jack hits the board somebody could have an upstairs wrap and you could be a gone goose. Naturally, you're never looking to make the bottom end of a straight, especially in a multiway pot.

You're looking to make a big flush with this hand and just hoping the board doesn't pair after you make it. Any time the board pairs in pot-limit Omaha, be very, very careful. It's like a red light suddenly flashing. When the board pairs in Omaha high-low, it's less serious because if three low cards are out there and you have the nut low, you can still win part of the pot. And high-low is a limit game: You can't get killed in it or in the limit high Omaha game, whereas you can get flat busted in pot-limit Omaha.

I recently saw two hands played in a big pot-limit ring game that illustrate this point. David "Devil Fish" Ulliott flopped three queens and Sammy Farquhar was in the pot with him. The flop came Q-8-2. Devil Fish led at it and Sammy called. On fourth street came a five. Devil Fish bet at it, Sammy raised, and Devil Fish called him.

Sammy didn't see that David had a $5,000 chip and so he just raised for the blacks that he saw in front of him. At the river came a nine. Sammy bet $3,400, the amount Ulliott had left. Devil Fish says, "You got a J-10 in your hand?" And I'm thinking, "Looks to me like Sammy had a queen and was trying to double-pair to win the pot playing in a short three-handed game, and ended up making the other straight that was possible (the 9-8-7-6-5)." And that's exactly what happened: He caught runner-runner and backdoored the straight to win the pot against the three queens.

Devil Fish went crazy. He said that the only thing he was hoping was that a nine, ten or jack didn't come on the end — because if Sammy had a Q-J-10-9, then he would have had a legitimate hand to play, you see. But the way some of those guys play at the big limits, they *don't* have a legitimate hand a lot of times.

This just shows how Murphy's Law works: Anything that *can* happen, *will* happen in Omaha. And it will happen even more often in limit high Omaha because players don't have to call as much money to draw. For that reason, more pots are played multiway in limit than in pot-limit.

Practice Hand 7

Omaha High-Low

I would just throw this hand away in Omaha split because there is no low draw. Our rule in Omaha high-low is to play hands that have scoop potential — but the only way you can scoop with this hand is on the high end. You could play it around back (on the button or one spot in front of it) in an unraised pot when you don't think it'll get raised. I wouldn't play it in a raised pot. You definitely would not play the A-6 for a low hand (for me, the A-4 is the worst low hand I want to draw to for low).

Pot-Limit Omaha

This isn't much of a hand, but it is a playing hand if it's suited and you can play it in an unraised pot. Obviously, what you're looking for is K-Q-J, three cards in your suit, or something like 8-7-5 (which would be a helluva flop).

A Q-J-8 would be another type of wraparound you'd like, but I don't want to see just a Q-J-X out there with no suits because then all I'd have is an open-end straight, and in Omaha I don't want just an open-end straight draw.

Other than flopping three of one of your cards, a flush, or catching the 8-7-5 or Q-J-8, the optimum drawing flop is one that has either a Q-J in it or an 8-7 in it plus two cards in your suit. That way, you have wraps. Even an 8-7-4 flop would be OK, especially if it also had two of your suit in it.

Limit High Omaha

I would always take a flop to this hand in limit high Omaha, even in a raised pot, because it can't cost me as much to see the flop as it might in pot-limit. If you get involved with this hand in pot-limit — if you come in early with it and then get raised — what do you do if you get raised? If you call the raise and don't flop to it, you've invested a lot of money. But in limit games, you've only invested one more unit and you can get away from it cheaply if you don't flop to the hand.

Practice Hand 8

Omaha High-Low

I would never voluntarily play this hand in the split game because it's a trap hand. If the flop comes A-6-small or if comes with an ace and one small overcard to your hand, you can really get trapped with the 3-4-5-5 looking for a deuce. So, the best thing to do is not even play it to begin with. Catching an ace-deuce on the flop is what you're looking for (and it happens sometimes), but that's too much to hope for.

I call this a trap hand because it seems that you invariably flop something to it and get caught up in the action. For example, what happens if you catch a five on the flop? Suppose the flop comes K-J-5. You have third set, which is always dangerous in any style of Omaha. If the board pairs, you're just hoping the other guy doesn't have a pair of kings or jacks. And if it doesn't pair, you sure don't want to see another high straight card on the turn. Your only out may be another five or runner-runner A-2 or 2-6 for a low straight in the split game, or even in pot-limit and limit high Omaha.

Suppose you're in the big blind with 3-4-5-5 and the flop comes 5-5-6, which means that there's a possibility of someone making a low on the turn or river. You're definitely going to lead with the hand — you have to get whatever you can out of it. Sometimes you'll see a player check a small full house on the flop in Omaha high-low when a low pair and another low card flop. There's no reason to give a free card in this situation because if you bet, they're going to call anyway — so why not make them pay? You always want to maximize every hand you play.

Pot-Limit Omaha

The only way that this hand would come up for me in pot-limit Omaha is if I'm in the blind or if I decide to call a single bet to take off somebody who I'm sure is playing a big pair. If you can isolate some of the big pairs, sometimes you can take a flop and win a big, big pot (this is one of the finer points of playing pot-limit). But this is not a hand that I recommend playing.

Limit High Omaha

You might take a flop to this hand in the limit game. If you don't hit the flop, you simply get rid of it.

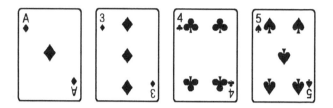

Omaha High-Low

Obviously, this is a pretty good eight-or-better hand. You have the second-nut low and the rundown cards, and you can't be counterfeited. A lot of times, an ace-trey will be the best low, especially at the higher limits. Your key cards are a deuce and a six and ideally, you'd like to see both of them come on the flop. Even better, you'd like to see two cards in your suit along with them.

Pot-Limit Omaha and Limit High Omaha

You can call the original bet with this hand, but you shouldn't call a raise with it. If the flop comes with little cards that connect, you're in pretty good shape.

When you play a hand like this, you're looking for a flop with a 2 and/or a 6 in it because those are your two key cards. Suppose the flop comes 2-4-5. Although you have the wheel, you could already be up against a six-high straight and drawing for your life trying to catch a six to tie for the high end of the pot ... unless the six makes an eight-high straight for somebody else!

Practice Hand 10

Omaha High-Low

Don't play this hand in Omaha split, period. This is strictly a losing hand.

Limit High Omaha

You can take a flop with this hand and hope to catch something to it ... a wraparound, a full house, anything you can get. A straight flush? Dreamer!

Pot-Limit Omaha

In pot-limit this is a takeoff hand, another hand similar to the 3-4-5-5 where you can beat those guys with the big pairs if a six or a low wrap comes on the flop. You can play it from around back, you don't want to stand a raise with it especially if you're heads-up because you know that your opponent is liable to have aces or kings or a big wrap up top double-suited.

The reason we're showing this hand double-suited is to demonstrate how having the low flush draw can really get you in trouble sometimes. You could make a seven-high flush in clubs or a six-high flush in hearts and be deader than a door nail. Actually, you don't want to have a flush draw with this hand; if that's all you have, get rid of it. But if you flop a straight or a set — a reason to stay in the hand — a backdoor flush could come in for you, and then you wouldn't necessarily need to have a big flush because backdoor flushes can be weaker and still win the pot. But the point is that you're never betting a flush draw as the optimum part of the hand.

The main strength of this hand and hands similar to it is its takeoff value against people who are playing big pairs in pot-limit Omaha. Suppose there's a little raise followed by three or four callers. In this case, there's nothing wrong with calling the raise because you know they most likely are all playing big cards and your little cards are probably live. After all, there are 52 cards in that deck — and you have a chance to take them off their big hands if you can catch the little cards.

Practice Hand 11

Omaha High-Low

The only way that you would consider playing this hand in the split game is when you're stiffed in in the big blind or little blind in an unraised pot ... period. Again, don't play the middle cards in this game. You have no way of scooping the pot unless the flop comes absolutely perfect for high and no low gets there.

Pot-Limit Omaha

This is just the normal type of decent rundown hand that you're trying to get a flop to in pot-limit. The general rule is that if there are three players in the pot in addition to you, you might stand a raise with this hand hoping that you flop a wrap. You could flop a lot of different cards where you have nut draws. Suppose the flop comes with a 6-5, 7-6, 8-6 or 9-6 — these are all bottom-end straight cards that you want to see. You don't want the top-end cards out there — if a Q-J comes down, you could be dead already — so you're always thinking of catching the bottom end to this hand.

Obviously, the best flop you could get is 6-5-4 in three suits, but catching it is very unlikely.

Limit High Omaha

You play this hand in about the same way you would play it in pot-limit. You can stand a raise with it suited or unsuited. If you don't flop to it, get rid of it. Suppose the flop comes with a J-7-4. You have an inside wrap to the J-7, but then suppose a queen comes off on the turn. Now you really don't know where you are in the hand. Somebody might have a wrap to the king and you're really in trouble. Get the drift?

You have to be very careful with this hand. You want to flop the low end of the straight because then you also will have the possibility of making an even higher straight if a higher card comes off that promotes the strength of your hand. Remember that you always want to be able to draw to a bigger hand than the one you have already made.

In the limit game you can play this type of hand stronger than you would in the pot-limit structure, and you also would play it longer. In pot-limit you might have to lay it down if the flop comes with two cards in a suit that isn't yours; otherwise it would be pretty hard to lay it down if two of your key cards come on the flop. Remember that in the limit game there are more cards that you can play deeper into the hand.

There are some flops that we haven't discussed that are obviously strong ones to this hand — it could come 10-10-9, 9-9-8, 9-9-7 ... and 10-10-10 would really be nice!

Practice Hand 12

Omaha High-Low

I don't like this hand in eight-or-better. You might take a flop to it hoping for high cards, but if the flop comes with low cards you must dump it. This isn't a hand that I would want to play from an early position, but I might play it from around back, particularly in a multiway pot.

If you're in the middle with three people already in the pot, you might call, figuring that most of them have come in with low cards. Once again, you have to size up your opponents and decide who is playing what. In the split game, it's very easy to size up the players because so many hands are shown down, but it's amazing how many people are staring into space or talking to somebody, not paying attention, when hands are turned over at the end.

Pot-Limit and Limit High Omaha

I like this hand. Now you're getting to the point where suits could come into play; however, if you made a flush you'd have to be very leery of it. You wouldn't want to lead with the flush, you would have to play it soft.

This is another good rundown hand and if you flop a wrap you'll be drawing at the nuts at all times, or you could flop the nuts. You also could flop two pair to the hand, of course. If the flop comes Q-J-2, for example, and there isn't much action you probably have the best hand. Somebody may have the big wrap to it, but even with two pair, you still have the bottom wrap. And if the turn came with an eight, you would have the nuts.

Practice Hand 13

Omaha High-Low

Obviously you take a flop to this hand in the split game. If the flop comes with little cards, you release the hand. And if it comes with big cards that give you a wrap or a set or a made straight, and it looks like you could scoop the pot, you play it strong. That's pretty cut and dried. Whenever you have a high hand in eight-or-better and the flop comes high, you play the hand the same way that you would play it in limit high Omaha.

If even one low card comes on the flop, some weak players with premium low cards will take a card off to try to catch runner-runner low cards — just one more reason to play strong when you catch a two-card high flop with this type of hand. Remember that more scooped pots are won by high hands when the board comes high than they are with nut-nut hands (the wheel and top flush, for example).

Pot-Limit and Limit High Omaha

This is a playing hand. If you catch a 10 on the flop and that's the top card on the board, you're in great shape. If the flop comes with a K-9 or an A-K you have the inside wrap. If it comes 9-8-7, that's terrific because you have the best hand with a draw to a higher hand.

The best possible flop would be 10-9-8, top set and a made straight. If it comes two of the same suit, you would play it soft. But wait — if it comes 10-9-8 with two suited cards, I don't see how you could play it soft! You *can't* because you still have top set and a made straight. You might get raised by the big flush draw but you sure as hell have to play it to see one more card at least.

If the flush draw makes the nuts on the turn, he's coming after you. Then, of course, you are no longer the favorite ... but stuff happens, you know. However, if there are only two flush cards on the turn, then you're a huge favorite.

Now suppose you catch this flop:

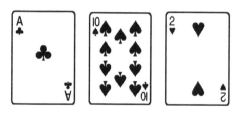

You're in a four-way pot and there has been action before the flop. You've flopped middle set and don't know where you are in the hand. This is a good example of when it comes down to playing the players. You look around and ask, "Who raises with aces before the flop? Who doesn't?" You know the answer because you have found it out during the play of the game.

Suppose you lead off with second set and a player who never raises with aces before the flop raises you. You *know* that he doesn't raise coming in with aces so that he doesn't tip his hand off. Now you're put to the decision as to whether or not he has three aces. Most of the time he would have them, especially with a broken board.

You can figure that your top players will not raise with the inside wrap on this type of flop, especially not with the ace looking them in the face. They might raise with a big wrap *before* the flop, but not *on* the flop because the ace is out there. So, what is your opponent raising with? This is where your playing skill comes in. These are the decisions for which you can't write down any cut and dried advice, it's just situational play that you have to make up your mind about.

When you're playing the limit high game, a lot of your straight cards may already be out if there was action before the flop. In a multiway pot, for example, the cards you need to make your high straight might not be available to you because they're already in other players' hands. You have to take this point into consideration.

For example, say that you play K-K-Q-J in a raised pot in a limit high Omaha game and they all come in. The flop comes A-10-7. Now you have to make up your mind as to whether any of your cards are still in the deck. In this hand with this flop, the pair of kings isn't even entering into the mix — it's the middle wrap that you're looking at.

Practice Hand 14

Omaha High-Low

The only time that this hand should be played in eight-or-better is when you're stiffed in in the big blind in an unraised pot. To continue past the flop would require a perfect scenario.

Pot-Limit Omaha

You can play this middle rundown hand in pot-limit but you don't want to stand a raise with it. If you can come in cheaply, why not try it? If you catch a flop to it, you're in hog heaven but if you don't, you dump it. Just remember that if you flop a straight to it with two of the same suit on the board and you get any action, don't be afraid to throw it away. Overall, this isn't a hand that I would feel very enthusiastic about.

Limit Omaha High

You can call a bet or a single raise with this hand in the high Omaha game. I might even come in with it from up front, but if I don't catch a big flop to it, I would throw it away. Suited or unsuited the hand plays the same.

You're not looking to make a flush since you don't have a nut-flush draw and almost any opponent could have a flush draw higher than yours (unless you flop a straight flush, of course). If you flop a straight to it, you would take off a card on fourth street even if the board is double-suited. After all, you have the nuts. Naturally, you don't want to flop a J-10-9, you want a baby flop. A flop like 10-9-5 is an OK flop, but remember that you can't get any bigger while somebody who's playing K-Q-J-10 has the top-end straight draw. The bottom line is that this is a playable hand in the limit game but you have to be careful with it.

Practice Hand 15

Omaha High-Low

You probably have to take a flop with this hand in the eight-or-better game, but this is a trap hand. If an ace hits on the flop, you have a low draw and nothing else ... no backup for your 2-3. You want to flop a king to it, of course, or an ace suited to two low cards in either clubs or hearts so that you have the nut-flush and the nut low on the flop. But don't count on it!

I'd probably call a bet with this hand before the flop, but I don't want to stand any raises with it. If an ace hits the board, your kings are nullified and then you're just playing for low. Actually, there are so many traps in this hand that I recommend you don't play it at all.

Pot-Limit Omaha

You have to take a flop to this hand but you do not raise with it and you don't want to stand a raise with it. You want to catch a king or an ace suited to one of your suits. But be very careful with this hand, especially in pot-limit. It's another one of those hands that could cost you a lot of money. With this hand, you can get broke and that's no joke.

Limit Omaha High

In the limit game you'll see a flop with the hand and then play it pretty much the same way you would in pot-limit.

A Trap Hand

Now let's take a look at a trap hand that I see being played in Omaha high-low, especially at the lower limits:

I've seen a lot of players come in with this type of hand, the K-Q-2-3 single or double-suited, particularly from around back in the low-limit split games. It might look playable, but the hand has no nut-flush cards and no backup to the 2-3. In fact, I can't think of any Omaha game that I would play this hand, either single or double-suited.

Practice Hand 16

Pot-Limit and Limit High Omaha

You'll see the flop in both the pot-limit and limit high games with this hand. In pot-limit you have a lot of possibilities with the hand. Flushes aren't something you're looking for, but a flush could win the pot if it came runner-runner on the turn and river when the nut flush isn't always out there.

Obviously, you want to flop a queen or rundown cards. You especially want to flop a 10, your key card, with at least one other straight card. Or flopping a split board like Q-7-2 would be pretty nice!

Omaha High-Low

I don't play this hand in eight-or-better. You have no chance at all for the low end and the pair of queens isn't one of the top two pair.

Practice Hand 17

Pot-Limit and Limit Omaha High

With only one gap, this is definitely a playable hand in the high games but I don't want to stand too much pressure with it. This is a pretty nice rundown hand but you need to hit perfect to it and I don't like any hand that I have to hit perfect.

An A-K is a good flop because nobody can make a higher straight, and a K-9 is ideal. If you flop a Q-J, you might not like it too much because even though you have top two pair, there probably would be all sorts of straight draws out against you. It's a hand that you have to be very careful with. You hope to flop the nuts and that no suits come out. This is just a medium quality hand way down in the rankings.

Omaha High-Low

This is not a hand that I recommend playing in the split game unless you're in late position in a multiway pot or are stiffed in with it in one of the blinds. As long as your high cards can connect with an ace, you're in jockeying position to win either the high end or possibly scoop the whole pot if an ace comes on the board and a third low card doesn't come. You want the ace on the board because without it you're probably not going to get any action. You'll see some players come in with this hand from up front, especially guys who usually play limit hold'em, but it's a trap hand. I don't like it in Omaha high-low because it's just too much trouble to bother with.

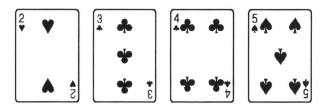

Omaha High-Low

You can play this hand in the split game in an unraised pot, but unless you catch the ace on the flop, this can really be a trap, *trap* hand. Let's say the flop comes 8-6-3. You have the low straight draw (and a pair) and that's fine ... but you only have the 2-4 for low. When the money starts going it, somebody's going to have A-2 and you'll be trailing all the way. Boy, that can be dangerous.

If there has been a lot of action before the flop, you pretty much know that either all or two/three of the aces are out, which decreases your chances of catching an ace on the flop. Some players like to play this hand in the right spot — they also like to play any four wheel cards, which isn't always such a bad idea. It's just that if you count the number of times that you'll flop to these types of hands versus the number of times that you don't, it doesn't measure up. That's why you always like to have an A-2 or A-3 in your low-draw hand so that if the flop comes with low cards, you have a good shot at it.

Pot-Limit and Limit High Omaha

I won't play this hand in the two high Omaha games. It's just too low a rundown hand.

Pot-limit Omaha and Limit High Omaha

This hand gives you a lot of opportunities to make the nuts in the high games. Look at it closely: You could catch a K-Q-10 or a 10-8-6 or a 10-8-X for a wraparound draw. You wouldn't necessarily want to catch a Q-10-8, although you'd have the nut straight at the moment, because you could be up against a straight draw with a king in it and get outdrawn.

You have the nut-flush draw if two clubs come on the flop, and a backdoor flush possibility if you consider the J-7 suited (in case one spade comes on the flop). If the flop came with two spades and nothing else that fit my hand, I would never play the J-7 for a flush draw, although I might call a bet.

The best feature of this hand is that you can flop a lot of straights to it that are nut straights. In a ring game, I would play it from up front. Of course, I'd have to decide in advance how much pressure I would be willing to take with it, but this is definitely a playing hand.

Omaha High-Low

I wouldn't play this hand at all in the eight-or-better game because I just don't see any value in it, certainly not enough to invest any money in it.

Practice Hand 20

Omaha High-Low

I don't play this hand at all in Omaha high-low, not even in a tournament. You have a jack-high flush possibility and could make some high straights, but you can get in a lot of trouble with this hand. It just isn't worth it.

Pot-limit and Limit High Omaha

In pot-limit and limit high Omaha where you only play high hands, a K-J-9-8 might be a playable hand. Obviously, if you don't flop to it, you can get away from the hand. I don't really consider the J-8 flush draw to be an important element in the hand, but if the flop comes with cards such as 10-7-X or Q-10-X, you have a big wrap with this hand.

Or if it comes with a 7-6-5 or 7-6-X, you have the upstairs wrap with it. So, it isn't really too bad a hand in either pot-limit or limit high, although I wouldn't want to have to stand a raise with it in pot-limit.

In limit high Omaha I might play this hand from any position. If I have limped in from a front or middle position, I would call a raise. In pot-limit you have to be more careful about your position when you play this type of hand because if you get raised you can get involved for a lot of money — and then you would have to flop the stone joint to the hand to continue further.

Practice Hand 21

Omaha High-Low

This is a hand that may have some value at a shorthanded table. You have two cards that work with big cards and you have three cards that work with small cards. A lot of times when you're playing shorthanded (four or fewer players), you aren't up against the nuts for the low. You also would not worry as much about drawing to a king-high flush in a shorthanded game as you would in a full ring game.

The optimum flop is 2-3-4, but 2-3-8 and similar flops also should be fine. A 3-4-7 would give you the nut straight and second-nut low on the flop. As I say, playing this hand shorthanded is acceptable, but the chances are high that you will get trapped with it in a full ring. You also might play the hand toward the late stages of a tournament, again in a shorthanded situation.

Pot-limit Omaha and Limit High Omaha

I don't give this hand any credence whatsoever in pot-limit. I just couldn't force myself to play it — I couldn't stand any action with it. If I get raised before the flop, what am I looking for? 2-3-4, 3-4-7, three cards of the same rank as any one of my cards (or two cards the same rank as one of mine and one card the same rank as one of my other cards) and that's about it. It has a little more value in limit than it does in pot-limit, but I'm going to let somebody else play this one! ♣

Chapter 6

THE TOURNAMENT TRAIL: TALES AND TACTICS

by T. J. Cloutier

This chapter is not entirely about how to win Omaha tournaments: It is more of a collection of observations and stories that have come up over the years.

Poker is a Game of Mistakes

All poker is a game of mistakes. No poker player plays perfectly on every hand, but if you let your opponents make the majority of mistakes, you're going to win the money. If everybody played alike, poker would just be a hand holding contest and the best hand would always win. Over a period of time, the cards would break even and nobody would be a winner. Everybody would be even. So, the idea of all poker games is to minimize the number of mistakes that you make.

For example, in a no-limit hold'em tournament that I recently played, the first man brought it for a raise and the second man reraised. I'm sitting right next to him and I have two aces. I move in. The first man throws his hand away and the second man calls with two queens when he has no chance, *no* chance. We were down to twelve players in the tournament and there was no way in the world that his two queens could be good after I had put in the third raise. But he called ... and doubled me up.

This is a perfect example of mistakes. You have to use your head in these situations. Anybody worth his salt knows better than to make that call. The fewer mistakes you make the better you'll come out at the end of the day, the month, the year. Over a year's time, mistakes are the dividing line between profit and loss. In the short run, of course, luck comes into the equation.

Remember this: A mistake that you make in a ring game where you can go to your pocket for more money will be magnified ten times in a tournament. It is ten times worse to commit that same mistake in a tournament as it is to make it in a cash game ... if you're trying to win the tournament. Now, if you're somebody who just wants to play, do what you want, but you aren't going to get there.

Small Rebuy Tournaments

People have asked me if they should take more chances in the small rebuy tournaments. I've seen some people playing real loose in those events, trying to get a hold of a lot of chips early, but I think that's wrong. I'll tell you why — you don't win the tournament in the first couple of hours and that's all there is to it. Nobody's ever won the tournament in the first three hours either. And that's how long many of the rebuy tournaments allow rebuys.

When you're starting out, you're putting up a certain amount to win a particular percentage over that. Every time you rebuy, you knock your percentage of win pool down a notch. I'm not saying *not* to rebuy, but if you rebuy you do it because you have had something legitimate beat, not because you gave it away. That's the only reason you're rebuying — because you lost your original buy-in when you got something beat. And make sure it was a *real* hand that got beat because if you had $500 to start with, and you've lost it, all you're getting in the rebuy is the $500 that you started with. It's not as though you're increasing your stack — you're right back on square one.

I'm all in favor of the add-on to increase your chips, but make sure you've had something beat before you make a rebuy. Try to play on that first buy-in, play it like you were playing a no-rebuy tournament. Why should you rebuy? Let the other players do that — they'll build the pot for you.

In some tournaments you can't rebuy until you run out of chips or fall below a certain amount. In others you can rebuy right away. If you're playing a *limit* tournament that has one optional rebuy and one add-on, and if you're planning on sacrificing, say, $1500 to the tournament, then I suggest rebuying right away and then taking the add-on. But I would never do it in pot-limit Omaha because of the beats you can take for your whole stack. You need the rebuy for your comeback stake.

Omaha High-Low Strategy

When I play in Omaha high-low tournaments, I usually won't play a hand like 2-3-4-5. I'll play it heads-up or three-handed, but in a full ring game I won't play it. I don't want to get stiffed — I don't want to get loser on a hand that I know I shouldn't have been in there with in the first place.

I've seen players in the low buy-in tournaments coming in with K-2-3-4 (one high card with three wheel cards). You can play some of these hands in some ring games: You've seen what the other players are playing and you can loosen up your action a little bit. But as far as the rules go for hands that you should play? The K-2-3-4 isn't one of them.

Neither is the 2-3-4-5. But I've played them, you've played them, we've all played them. Say that you're playing in a tournament and you start with $500. They're playing at the

$30-$60 limit. This hand could end up taking half of your chips very easily. So you ask, "Do I want to risk half my chips on this piece of cheese?" So you don't do it — that's the way to play.

This is the point that Tom and I stressed so much in our first book — in tournaments you can't go back into your pocket, so when you play a hand you'd better damn well like the hand. And you'd better have it in a good spot, because otherwise it could cost you a lot of chips ... chips that are very hard to recover.

I try to have more money at each level of the tournament. I don't care how much the increase is, I know that if I increase my stack at every level I have a chance to win the tournament. So, I let a lot of people do a lot of things that they want to do and I play *my* way. My way is not to get involved with hands that might eat up my chips.

Get involved when you're doing the betting, when *you* have the power, not when *they* have it. If you have the patience to wait for the good hands, they will come sooner or later. In a recent no-limit tournament, I didn't hold aces or kings during the first six hours. Then in the next two rounds at my table, I held them once in each round.

Bad Beats

In tournaments, you have to expect bad beats and learn to take them without going on tilt. Sometimes, that's hard to do. Late in the no-limit hold'em championship tournament at the Carnivale of Poker, with four tables left, I had $38,000 in chips. A man brought it in for a modest raise and I called with A♥ Q♥ in the big blind. The flop came Q-3-2 in three suits. I led out with a $6,000 bet and he moved in on me. I knew I had the best hand so I beat him into the pot.

He says, "You've got me. I'm bluffing" and turns over the J♠ 9♠. An eight came on the turn and a ten came at the river to give him a straight! If I'd won the hand, I would've had the lead in the tournament — instead, I was out of it.

So, here's an unofficial "tip from the top:" That's the way it goes — first your money, then your clothes!

Here's another tip: A lot of limit hold'em tournament players are taking a shot at no-limit hold'em tournaments these days. The small, rebuy, no-limit tournaments are popular events in a lot of cardrooms because they give people a chance to practice big-bet poker skills. Remember that limit players are usually *one-bet* players. They tend to put their chips all-in a lot of the time. If you're an experienced no-limit or pot-limit player you have to take this tendency of theirs into account in your strategy, because these players have the same tendency to push in all their chips in pot-limit Omaha tournaments.

The Morning Glories

Once again let me stress that in tournaments you can't go to your pocket. Every time you put chips in a pot you should know that you have a pretty good chance of banking a profit. But there are a lot of "morning glories" in tournaments who don't understand this concept. If a race horse works out at 12 seconds per furlong, that's considered to be a real good workout, so if they go three furlongs in 36 seconds, that's very good. A "morning glory" might run those three furlongs in 34 seconds ... and that's flying. So the guys at the track will bet 'em down like hell when they see those workout stats. But he's only good in the morning — he runs dead last in the afternoon.

Believe me, the same thing holds true in poker tournaments. Morning glories are players who get a lot of chips early in the tournament but who have no chance of winning it. For this reason, you should not worry about how many chips other people have early in the tournament. Play the way that you're supposed to play and you have a chance to get there. If you don't, you probably won't.

I've already told the story about the player who was in a major tournament in Southern California, but it bears repeating. At the end of the first hour, this man had $50,000 in chips, five times the amount he'd started with. He had made every draw he could possibly make. He did *not* make it to the second limit change!

He was the epitome of the morning glory. He kept playing the same way he had been playing very early and, suddenly, the percentages caught up with him and he couldn't make a hand. "This is what happens with morning glories," Tom adds. "They get a lucky rush of cards early, or play some substandard starting hands that get there, and they don't adjust their play once they get a lot of chips. More often than not, they self-destruct."

Playing at the World Series

When Dana interviewed me about the 1998 World Series championship event when I came in third to Scotty Nguyen and Kevin McBride, she mentioned that people had commented on how calmly I had handled myself at the final table when I raised with K-Q three-handed and McBride called with J-9 and busted me.

"I couldn't believe that McBride would make that call for $120,000 and then put in another $450,000," Tom said. First of all, an experienced player might have called the $10,000 or so that was in there instead of making it $40,000. He definitely would not have called a reraise of $120,000, no other player in the world would have done that. So I knew that I had the best hand. And I knew I had the best hand after the flop, too. But that's poker, you know, and that's how McBride got there. When the commentators talked about the final-table play, they hadn't seen the hands that I threw away at the final table.

For example, a hand came up when Scotty made a $40,000 raise, a standard raise at that point. Kevin called the $40,000 raise. I had two jacks in the big blind and made it $200,000 to go. Scotty threw his hand away and Kevin came back over the top of me for all of his chips. I took a long time on this hand, the longest I've taken in quite a while. Finally, I thought, "He's been playing every hand from behind, check-raising every time he has a big hand. He's got me beat." I threw in the two jacks and he showed me two kings.

"It's pretty hard to throw away two jacks three-handed, isn't it?" Dana asked. Yes, it is. Then about a half an hour later, the same thing happened again. Scotty made it $40,000, Kevin called the $40,000, and again I had two jacks in the big blind. This time I decided to just flat call and see the flop. It came 8-7-2, three suits. Scotty checks, Kevin checks, and I bet $20,000 ... just a little test bet. I was supposed to have the best hand, judging from the way the play had come down. Scotty passed and Kevin raised me $200,000 and I threw the jacks away. Once again, he showed me two kings. That was twice that I threw away two jacks in situations where they were so hard to get away from it's out of this world.

"But you knew the guy was check-raising with his big hands, right?" Tom asked. Well, I knew that any time that he was betting money from behind, he was a lot stronger than he was when he was leading with a hand. For example, another hand came up in an unraised pot. I had a 10-9 in my hand and the board came J-10-3. Kevin made it $20,000 on the flop. I called him, Scotty called him. On fourth street came a deuce. He bet $20,000 again. I knew that I had the best hand, so I called him. Scotty called him. I knew Scotty had a straight draw, the way this hand was coming up.

I thought, "Let this board pair deuces or come with a four or five, something like that, and I'll win this pot for sure." Well, the board paired deuces. Here he came, $20,000 again. I called and Scotty threw his hand away (he had the straight draw, just as I had thought). And I thought that Kevin had been betting third pair, and that's exactly what he was doing ... he had a three in his hand.

"Had you ever seen him play before the World Series?" Dana asked. I had watched him the day before. Even though he wasn't at my table, I kept leaning over in my seat watching him when he was holding all those cards over Bobby Hoff. Kevin might have deuces or treys or fours and the board might have an A-K-8 on it and he would lead at it on the flop. I made up my mind right then about what kind of player he was, what he would do. He liked to lead small at pots, hoping that he could trip up on something. I used that information all the way through. These are things that veterans will think of that a lot of other players won't think of.

"Couldn't he have tricked you by accident?" Tom asked. " Suppose he had slipped in with an A-8 suited when you had the two jacks and thought that he had the best hand." No ... he wouldn't play that hand that way, so don't get me wrong ... but I made a definite decision that he had me beat at the time. It seemed that he would call bets — say the flop came with an 8-7-3 or whatever — he would either call or lead with it. And he wouldn't raise on the flop. I'm not saying that he wouldn't raise on fourth street if another little card came, but he would never raise with the kings on the flop. So when I laid down the jacks, my first instinct was that he had them beat and that I might get a better situation to get my money in, and I wasn't near broke.

"You know you're getting lucky when you take the worst hand and you draw out and make it," Dana commented. I know of only one time during the entire four days of the big tournament when I got either all my money or a major part of it in the pot with what probably wasn't the best hand. The flop came Q-9-8. I raised with a Q-10 and Ben called it. I made queens and tens and although I never saw his hand, everybody told me that he had an A-Q. That was the only time in the tournament when I got a large amount of money in with the worst hand. I'm not saying that I didn't make a little baby call here and there and get beat. But for any amount of money that mattered, this was the only time that I got my money in bad (and I still couldn't get broke with the hand). Until we hit the final table, I increased my money at every level.

"How do you explain weak players or inexperienced players winning big tournaments? What happens that makes it possible?" Dana asked. This is only the second time it's ever happened at the World Series (the other time was when Hal Fowler won it against Bobby Hoff back in 1979). But Kevin McBride is a much better player than Fowler was, and in fact, he's a much better player than most people give him credit for. I mean, he got away from some hands and things like that. He won the $1,500 no-limit tournament at the Rio after he came in second at the World Series, you know.

But Kevin also caught a lot of cards for four days straight. He called Bobby Hoff with two queens for his last $200,000 with an ace on the board on fifth street. And it broke Bobby. But I'll tell you, Bobby would make that play again and so would I, the way it came down. The only reason that I probably wouldn't have done it at that time is because Kevin had beaten Bobby three big pots in a row before that. So, Kevin probably called because he thought that Bobby was stealing. And indeed he was, representing the ace.

Another key pot had come up before that one. Bobby has A-K and raises it and Kevin calls him with K-10. The board comes three rags and then a king comes on fourth street. Bobby makes a decent bet and Kevin calls him. Off comes a ten on fifth street. Now Bobby makes a big bet and Kevin comes over the top of him. Bobby had $800,000 with three tables to go ... as far as I was concerned, he was going to be at the final table. He's one of the greatest hold'em players who's ever lived, OK? But Kevin beat him four pots in a row and took the whole $800,000 away from him! When things like that happen for you, you know that things are going pretty good for you.

"So you're saying that if a less experienced or less skilled player shows well in a tournament, it's probably because he got lucky on his big draws?" Dana surmised. Yes. And I've seen top players get huge amounts of chips early and then blow them just as fast as they won them. I've seen Stuey Ungar do it and I've seen Phil Hellmuth do it — when the cards stop coming to them, they still think they can run over the table. They don't slow down

That was Stuey's only fault in tournaments and it's Phil's biggest fault. I've talked and talked to Phil about it, saying "Phil, you just can't run over every game you play in." He had $170,000 on the second day of the WSOP a few years ago and when he got down to $110,00 he called me over and asked, "What am I doing wrong, T. J.?" I said, "Phil, you can't raise every pot and run over everybody. Slow down. Some of these guys can play hold'em, you know. You'd better learn to give them credit."

Tournament Structure

I liked the tournament structure that they used to have at Caesars Palace. In the no-limit hold'em tournament the first buy-in was $220 with $20 juice. The first rebuy cost $500. After that, any subsequent rebuys cost $1,000 and you got the same number of chips that you paid for. The rebuys were unlimited. So you got $500 in chips for your first $200, then you got $500 for your second ... and then you got $1,000. It was a great structure.

I don't mind making the rebuys because I love to see the pot build up. I'm one of those guys who wants the pot to get as big as it can get when I play, that's all there is to it. I hate playing in one of these tournaments like I did like night at the Legends of Poker when I won $1,500 for a $120 buy-in and I had to play until 3:30 in the morning.

Of course, the only reason I played it was for the points ... I got 55 points for first place. The Bicycle Club gives a best all-around player award for the tournament and you get points based on finishing in the top 16 players. Mel Judah came in second on the first day and played the $50 mixed-double tournament and got points for it, and the next day he won the $50 hold'em event. After the first two events, he had 87 points and I hadn't even played in one yet.

Then I came in second in the third event, and he came in fourth for over 100 points. He was in the money again yesterday so now he has 122 points ... and I'm up to 102 points and he can feel me breathing down his neck ...

Intuition in Tournaments

You often play by your intuition at the final table and do things that you don't do while you're just still trying to get there. At the final table you loosen up a little bit in spots against shorter stacks and things like that, things that you can't do on your way to the final table.

When you read about the hands that were shown down at the final table, a lot of times they just look like trash. But because the blinds are so high, you have to adjust your starting hand standards to what it's costing you for every round at the table — and it's costing you a hell of a lot of money each round — and so you're forced to play a few more hands.

I don't know exactly what the blinds were when we finished the pot-limit Omaha tournament at the 1998 World Series of Poker, but you can bet that they were high enough that at any one time you could have gotten all the money in. There was about $340,000 in chips at the final table and yet the blinds were high enough that you had to play. At the finals of the 1998 eight-or-better event, there was $408,000 in chips on the table.

When the blinds become extremely high, some of the hands that were marginal early in the tournament become acceptable to play late in the event. You just can't wait for the nuts when the blinds are burning up your chips. You have to be selective when you play these hands, of course, but you have to play them.

Playing Side Action During Tournaments

My bread and butter used to be the no-limit hold'em games but now those games have all dried up and there's nothing around home to play. I started playing the tournament circuit and did well, so I stayed with it, but I don't consider myself to be a tournament specialist like Tom. I don't care whether I play in tournaments or ring games, but I don't think the two mix very well. I don't believe that you can give yourself 100 percent to a tournament if you're also playing a lot of side action, and vice-versa. Although side action is what we all did for a good number of years, there are so many tournaments these days that a lot of us don't have time to play the side games anymore.

Occasionally, you can play side games and tournaments too, but believe me when I tell you that it usually takes all of your energy to play a tournament. You have to concentrate very hard and you're playing for a lot more money than you usually can make in a side game. Compared to the amount of money that you're risking, the amount of money that you can win in a tournament is so much higher than what you can win in most side games, that it takes all of your concentration to do well.

Then when you get into a side game where you know that you can win four or five thousand, you don't always have the total concentration that you need to win because you've already used up so much of it in the tournament. I think that a person can focus on something for only so long and then your brain has to have some time off. And that is why some tournament players don't do well in the side games. They don't play side games very often and when they do play them, they aren't giving them their full concentration.

This also is why some top tournament players have an avocation outside of poker, something else that they enjoy doing. Sometimes it's backgammon, like it is with Tom, or my marriage and golf, like it is with me. You need another outlet to stay balanced.

Getting a Track Record

People have asked me what it takes to be successful on the tournament trail, suggesting such things as concentration, motivation, skill and a big bankroll. You need those first three items in big doses, of course, but you don't necessarily need a big bankroll.

It costs a lot of money to play tournaments, that's true, but if you can establish a track record — become very successful in your tournament play — you won't have to worry about the money part. You'll get phone calls all the time from people who want a piece of your tournament action, so the money part will take care of itself. For the past 15 years I haven't been to a single tournament that I couldn't come into town without a dime of my own and still play it if I wanted to.

But if you're not successful at tournament play, I don't care if you're the greatest player in the world in the ring games, you're still going to have a hard time finding a backer. You have to show a track record on the tournament trail.

The 1998 Pot-Limit Omaha Championship Event

At the Four Queens one year, we got down to the final four in the no-limit hold'em event, Doyle Brunson, Chip Reese, Erik Seidel and me. That was the toughest final table I've ever played in any tournament. During the World Series in 1998, we got down to the final three in the pot-limit Omaha event and once again it was Doyle and Erik and me. I thought it was quite a coincidence that the three of us were facing off again in a big event.

The lineup also included David Mosley, a very tough player from England, and Donnacha O'Dea, an excellent player from Ireland. Patrick Bruell, the movie star from England, played great, absolutely great, and so did Mattie Kuortti (he never got out of line). Gary Haubelt played his usual solid game and Paul Rowe's also a good all-around player, so we had a very strong, solid lineup at the final table.

I went into it in the lead and Doyle was in second place. It was Erik Seidel who made the big comeback in that one — he started off in last chip position with only $8,500 and moved up to win third place. I took the worst of it in two or three pots, knowing that I had the worst of it. But I had such a chip lead on the rest of the players that I could take a few chances trying to knock somebody out. For most of the tournament I basically had let the other players knock each other out, but at the final table I took the job into my own hands. A lot of times, that's the way you have to do it when you're the one who has the big stack.

Somebody said something about the others being intimidated by Doyle and me because we were "big players with big stacks" in front of us. But I never feel intimidated by another player. I think Doyle's a fabulous player and has been one for years and years, but he can't intimidate me and I'm sure that I don't intimidate him.

On the end I offered to make a deal with Doyle based on the chip count. His reply was, "If I get to where we have an even chip count, maybe we can talk then." He was at a disadvantage in the chip count since he was about $50,000 behind me and he didn't want to get less than half of the pot. And I don't blame him — I don't like to make deals and I haven't offered them to very many players. I knew that there wasn't even a fraction of play between the two of us that was much different. We both could reel it in and we both could throw it out. As it turned out, I won it for $136,000 with no deal and Doyle took second money, $78,200.

It was a funny tournament in a way ... pot-limit events are usually that way. A lot of people were doing a lot of re-buying early and there was a lot of jostling around. We had players like Lindy Chambers and O'Neill Longson in it, men who can really play the game but who like it so much that they sometimes get into it real deep.

I also was at the final table of the $2,000 Omaha high-low event at the '98 Series where I finished fifth for $18,000 and change. Chau Giang, an excellent high-limit split player who won the lowball title a few years back at the Series, won it and Carl Bailey from Oklahoma took second. Brian Nadell is a top player who came in third. Of course, all of the top players are always at the World Series so there's never an easy field. And all the big players play all the tournaments, not just a few of them like you see happening in so many of the smaller buy-in tournaments. ♣

Herve Villechez, star of "Fantasy Island," playing with T. J. at the Golden Nugget's Pro-Celebrity tournament in 1985.

Jack Keller, Johnny Chan, Berry Johnston and T. J. Cloutier, the grand ol' team that was sponsored by Grand Casinos at the Bicycle Club's Tag Team Challenge tournament in 1993.

Chapter 7

TALES FROM T. J.

"Along the Road to the World Series of Poker"

The thing that's missing in the poker world these days (or is dying out fast) is all the characters from the past who were such colorful guys. When people ask me about the young players coming up today, I mention that they don't have the style the old guys had. Here are stories about a few of the gamblers I used to play with in Texas and Las Vegas.

Tippy Toe Joe Shotsman

In our first book, I told the story about George McGann robbing a poker game after he got loser and nobody saying anything about it when he came back and played the next day. Now let me tell you the story about George and Joe Shotsman ... they called him Tippy Toe Joe and he was an old-time poker player and a real heavy drinker back in Dallas. Tippy Toe Joe could drink more booze and still play poker than any man I've ever seen in my life. He made Bill Smith look like a piker!

Tippy Toe would come in and start playing at 2:00 in the morning after all the bars had closed. They took a water glass and just filled it with whiskey, and he'd drink it like he was drinking water ... and still play. He and George used to play head-up no-limit hold'em.

In this game, they'd been playing for about two weeks straight and Tippy Toe had beat George every time they played ... he was a much better player. But remember that George was a stone killer and always carried his gun. He was the type of guy who would meet you face to face and shoot you. If he had to shoot somebody, he'd look 'em right in the eye and then shoot 'em. Well, Tippy Toe breaks George again. So George pulls out his gun and says, "Tippy Toe, I want all the money you've got in front of you and all the money you've got in your pocket. This thing's over with and I'm getting some of my money back!"

So Tippy Toe pushes over his money and then reaches in his pocket where he has $10,000 in $100 travelers checks. George makes Tippy Toe sign every one of those travelers checks! Tippy Toe is pretty smart, so as he's signing these checks, he says, "Now George, this is gonna leave me awful short. Do you think you could let me keep about $3,000 so I'll have a little money on me?" Well, he talked George into loaning him back $3,000 of the money he's stealing from him!

After this is all done and they're going down the stairs from this joint, Tippy Toe looks up at George and he says, "George, we're not gonna let this little incident stand in the way of our poker game, are we?" And that's a true story. Tippy Toe didn't want to lose George — he knew he could beat him every time they played.

A Killer of a Poker Game

McGann was a killer for hire, but he wasn't the only one who played with us. He wasn't a very big guy, he always wore a suit and he had two guns. In the same game in Dallas there was R. D. Matthews who used to be Benny Binion's body guard. He always had a gun on him, but his big thing was hitting 'em with a baseball bat.

And there was Troy Inman, a killer who wouldn't want to face you. If he was going to kill you, he'd stand around the corner and get you as you went by. Then there was Haroldson,

who killed that judge, Judge Woods, down in San Antone —
he played in the game.

Now, they didn't all play at the same time, but they all
played in that same game. They were some real characters.
I'll never forget the time when I went there for the first time.
I knew who Troy was and he was running the poker game. I
won about $9,000 and he paid me off. Then he says, "Now,
T. J., this is a bad area so I'll walk you down the stairs and see
that you get to your car." I was more afraid of getting robbed
by him than I was by anybody else!

Bill Smith & Corky & Ike

Bill Smith was a world champion and he ended up playing $4-$8 hold'em at the Gold Coast poker room in his last
days. But Bill Smith was one of the greatest poker players
that ever lived. He was too tight when he was sober, but when
he got halfway drunk, he was the best player you've ever played
against. And if he got completely drunk, he just gave away his
money. You could always tell when Bill was past that halfway
point. If you were backing Bill Smith and you could just get
him halfway drunk, you knew you were gonna win money.
But he tipped you off in two different ways when he was totally drunk. Say the flop came out there with a 10-7-4. He'd
say, "21!" He'd start totalling the flop. Then when he got up
to get another drink or go to the bathroom, he'd have a little
hip-hop in his step. When he did that, you knew he was gone
and that was when you started playing with Bill. You knew
that he was gonna bluff every pot, it didn't matter what he
had. And he never slowed down — he'd just bluff, bluff, bluff.

I used to stake Bill when he was down on his luck back
in Dallas. And he wouldn't bluff anybody but me! He said he
could bluff me because I was staking him. Sooner or later,

you get a little tired of that and you just take him off and save what money's left, you know.

He was a character. There were these two guys: Corky Stiles and Ike White, a real nice black man who always played with us in the poker games in Dallas. Bill would get drunk in a game and lose his money and he'd say, "Give me $500, Corky." And Corky would slide him over $500. Bill would lose it in the first hand and then he'd say, "Give me $500, Ike." He'd lose it in the first hand. Then he'd go up to a thousand. He'd say, "Corky, give me $1,000." Corky would say, "Well, Bill, I'm getting a little short." And Bill would go, "I said, give me a thousand!" And they'd shove it over to him. Bill wasn't a mean guy, but he'd get belligerent when he just wanted to play.

He traveled that Southern circuit all the time ... he was in Corpus and San Antonio, Victoria and Houston. He played everywhere in Texas, but when I knew Bill he was just playing in Dallas. We played Wassahatchee, Corsicana and Dallas, a little triangle where the farthermost place away was around 45 miles. Bill could play. I met Joy through Bill's ex-wife, Cleta. That was the only blind date I ever went on and I ended up marrying the girl.

He used to go out every week night and drink. We used to go down to a place called The Towers in Dallas. There was this bar in there and all the rounders were there. Monday through Friday night after the poker, Bill would do down there religiously. But he never went on the weekends. So somebody asked him one time why he never went out on the weekends. "Well," he said, "holidays and weekends are amateur nights. *Real* drinkers go out during the week."

The Fights at Shreveport

One time I went down to Shreveport to see Sugar Ray Leonard fight Tommy Hearns and we went to Earnest's Supper Club for dinner, the greatest food in the world. After dinner we were going out to the fairgrounds to see the fight. We drove 200 miles from Dallas to do this. And who am I there with? R. D. Matthews, Henry Bowen and Troy Inman — three of the biggest rounders that ever lived. Henry's the one who did eight years on death row for something he didn't do. But can you imagine going there with those three guys? You talk about a fish out of water, I was really out of water. But I sure felt safe.

You hear about these gangs today? There isn't a one of those guys that this bunch would put up with. They'd look you in the face and shoot you just as soon as spit on the street. I mean they were some tough customers.

Ernest's Supper Club had the greatest food you've eaten in your whole life. When I was younger and lived in Shreveport, I had a charge account at Ernest's and I was one of the guys running the crap game upstairs at the club. If I didn't have any money I'd just sign my name for the food. Every time I walked in they had a band playing on the dance floor and they'd stop playing what they had been playing, and they'd start up with "I'm just a gigolo, everywhere I go." Every time I'd walk in the door, I tell you! But I loved to dance and I'd get out there and dance all I could every time I could.

The Poker Games in Dallas

These guys I played with in Texas were all great poker players but they didn't want to just play against each other. You always need producers to feed a game, you know. At one time we had three multi-millionaires playing in the game who would start the game and finish it.

One of them took the cure and joined Gamblers Anonymous and now he's a bigwig in G.A. And if Hugh Briscoe, who used to have all that land up in Denton, got broke he'd just sell another bit of land so he'd have more poker money. I guess he probably lost $10 million in Dallas. And then there was Ken Smith, who could play but was always on a time schedule so his money wasn't worth anything. He only had two hours for poker so he tried playing fast. But when Kenny wanted to, he could really play.

And then we got busted in Dallas and that was the end of the poker there. Now they have limit games all over town but it's nothing like it used to be. Somebody asked me if there are still games where you can go in and make a killing. Well sure ... there's enough poker rooms in California to choke a hog. Of course, the whole theory of having a cardroom these days is to never spread a big game — you don't want anybody to ever get broke because you want to keep the drop. In this one little town in California there's a cardroom with four or five tables in it but the most they ever get going is two games and $4-$8 is the top limit. (This is quite common in many of the smaller clubs.)

Bobby Chapman &
the Three Pizza Men

Bobby Chapman was the boss gambler in Dallas for years and years. He's the one who always put up the money for Art Saling's Omaha game, guaranteed the money for the game and all that. In this particular game, we were playing at the Ramada Inn that Art Saling managed and that's why we had the game there. Three guys who owned pizza places came over to play. This was the first time they'd played with us and they were horrible players. We were playing a big game with $25-$25-$50 blinds ... a really big pot-limit Omaha game ... when this pot came up.

Every poker game in Dallas or Fort Worth always kept at least one six pack of Schlitz beer in the refrigerator in case Bobby Chapman showed up. He might not play for three months but if he showed up, he was gonna drink ... and he would get bombed after his first beer. I mean, he just couldn't handle alcohol at all. His whole theory of playing poker and playing drunk was, "I'm gonna put enough money on the table that if I beat you one out of five hands, I break you." And he was a dog on most of 'em. When he was sober he played pretty good Omaha. He didn't play very good hold'em but he played damned good Omaha.

So, this funny hand came up. I'm on the button so I'm dealing. The first pizza man calls, another pizza man calls, and here comes Bobby Chapman and he raises it. Then the third pizza man calls. I'm on the button with 10-9-8-8 with one suit and I decide, "Well, Chapman's liable to be raising with anything and there's a lot of money in the pot. I might be able to win something here." So I reraise the pot about $1,200. Pizza man calls, second pizza man calls it, Bobby studies a long time ... and then he just flat calls it. Third pizza man calls.

When Bobby took a long time on it, I'm thinking, "He's got a big hand, a pair of aces. He's trapping in this hand." Here comes the flop: A-8-8. I flopped four eights in this pot! First pizza man checks, second pizza man checks, Bobby moves in. Third pizza man folds. "I think I'll call you, Bobby," I say.

There's over $28,000 in this pot and he never knew what hit him! This was the one time when Bobby was drunk and really had a hand. You see, a lot of times when he was drunk he'd bet all the way through and on the end he'd say, "Straight flush!" That meant he didn't even have a pair. Of course, Bobby's such a man he never said a word, just "You've got a pretty good hand there, T. J."

Chapman, What a Man!

Bobby used to always bring Nicholas, his big German shepherd, with him to the games. I'll tell you what a man he is, what a great guy he actually is. He got involved in a big, big game during the summertime one year and they flat cheated him out of $800,000. There were a couple of card thieves in the game and they cheated him out of that much money. Bobby came to us and said, "I know I got cheated out of that money, but I was fool enough to go for it. I lost the money so I'm paying it." And he paid off every dime he owed right away.

Then he stood good for Art Saling's game and at one time, three people were in over $150,000 in this one game. One of the guys who was in for $150,000 was one of the men who had been in with the two other thieves on stealing the money from Bobby in that poker game. When the game was over, this guy didn't have the money to pay off. Even after being cheated out of $800,000, Bobby still paid off the game, made it good.

And you know how this guy was paying him off? $2,000 a month. Unless you have so much money it doesn't matter, you'll never realize the whole $150,000 when you're getting paid only $2,000 a month. Hell, he could have had the $150,000 in the bank and made more interest on it than that. But he accepted that ... that's what a man he was. Most people who had just been cheated would've said, "Take a long walk on a short pier."

Troy Inman and Bob Yeager

As I mentioned before, when I played at the AmVets I was more afraid of getting robbed with Troy escorting me downstairs than I was afraid that somebody would be waiting for me with a gun. Of course, Troy's dead now. First of all, he had diabetes or something like that and his big toe fell off. Later, he died. Troy had ol' Bob Yeager scared. Bob was an ol' gambler and a gin cheat. Troy had Bob so afraid of him that Troy would call him on the phone when he was on short money and say, "I need a coupla thousand dollars," and Yeager was afraid to refuse him. Of course, if Troy had the money he would pay you back — it's not that he was a stone stiff. He was a killer but he wasn't a stiff.

Bowen Takes a Bad Beat

Henry Bowen was a real tough guy and a great poker player. In his younger days he was in prison a lot for bank robbery and just from being a super tough guy. And he had little dainty hands ... I could never understand how he could be so tough with those little dainty hands.

One Saturday we went to a rodeo in Tyler, Texas — Henry and I went with Johnny Wheeler, who ran the rodeo, and it was going on the next weekend as well. Well, I didn't go to the rodeo that next weekend, but Henry did. Hundreds of witnesses placed him at the rodeo at 11:00 p.m. in Tyler, Texas. Three people, a dope dealer and two others, were murdered by the side of a pool in Oklahoma City at 11:45 p.m.. And Henry got charged with the murder.

He was convicted of their murders and sat on death row for seven years. Benny Binion went to bat for him, paying for lawyers and other stuff, because he was a friend of Henry's. Finally, after his story came out on "60 Minutes," the case was retried and Henry was set free. He had been railroaded in this case because of the things he'd done in the past.

Henry and the Big Texan

So Henry had just gotten out of prison after being on death for seven years and he comes to the poker game run by the Big Texan I told you about in my first book (Henry hated the Big Texan). Now, you can imagine that you might be a little nervous about things if you've been away for seven years.

He's playing in our game and makes a bet and the Big Texan raises him. Henry's thinking about calling the raise and his hand is shaking a little bit. So the Big Texan says, "How come your hand's shakin', Henry?" to give him the needle while he's thinking about the call. So Henry very quietly turns to the Big Texan and says, "You know, ever since I got out of prison I've been trying to act like a Quaker, you know, tryin' to be nice to everybody. But there's a fine white line and you've just about stepped over it."

And I mean to tell you, the Big Texan went absolutely white, like a ghost. Henry was not the man you wanted to give a hard time to. The Big Texan went in the front room and watched television for about an hour ... he was scared to death that Henry was going to kill him.

Behavior in Poker Games, Then and Now

Some of these things that people do nowadays in the poker tournaments — act up and stuff like that — if they weren't killed, they'd have been beaten half to death if they had been playing in Texas in the old days. People wouldn't stand for that kind of behavior back then. There are a lot of hot-blooded players out there today. Sometimes, I get pretty hot inside myself but I'm not gonna show it. I might mumble once in a while but that's as far as I'm gonna go.

Years ago, Mr. Brooks told us, "If I thought that even one of those other ten players would feel sorry for me, I'd cry every time I had a bad beat, but I know they're all trying to beat me so I'm not gonna show my ignorance." And I've never forgotten that.

The Owl from Oklahoma

Bobby Baldwin played mostly in Oklahoma but he came down to Dallas and played with us a lot of times. When he was playing poker full-time, he was a great player. Of course, now he's a casino executive and has turned into a pretty tight player. They called him "The Owl" for just one reason — he was the best reader of a hand of anybody. You know how an owl's supposed to be real wise. Bobby Hoff used to say that Bobby was a 15 percent better poker player than any man alive. And that's quite a compliment. If someone is even one percent better, that's something ... 15 percent better is pretty strong. Even as a kid, Bobby was always a good player. He taught a course in poker one year at Tulsa University. It was an elective class with Bobby Baldwin, professor.

Doyle, Johnny, Slim and Sailor

Doyle and Slim and Sailor and Johnny were the big names in poker in those days. Sailor Roberts was a famous player who did more for down and out players than anybody else. If a guy was down on his luck, it was nothing for Sailor to give him a bankroll at any time. Sailor could do more with a 4-5 than any man alive. He'd show you that 4-5 three or four times and the next time he raised you'd think he had it again ... and he'd have those two eyeballs!

Sailor loved the girls and the parties. One time he went to San Angelo and beat that game out of $85,000 over about a three-month period ... and it was a small game, a $5-$10 pot-limit hold'em game. And when he left town he had less money than he'd brought to town with him — that's how much he liked to party with the girls. This happened when he was older.

I mean, he was a party animal. He just loved three things: playing golf and poker, and going out with the girls. And boy, they took him for every dime he had. I liked the girls, too, but I wasn't into hookers or anything like that ... but Sailor liked any kind of girl. Where he was a takeout specialist in the poker, they were taking him off ... they were a little sharper than he was. And he knew it but he didn't care — he just wanted to live life to the fullest.

Just ask Bobby Hoff and Carl McKelvey and Steve Lott and all those guys how many people Sailor helped out during his lifetime. He helped Bill Smith a thousand times if he helped him once. Because there was one thing about Bill — he could never stay in money.

The Cowboy and The Queen

I was watching a no-limit hold'em game at the Horseshoe a few years back, a $50-$50-$100 blinds game. Cowboy Wolford was playing and I was sitting behind him. When the dealer dealt the hands out, she exposed a queen. The hand still went and the queen was used for the burn card. The pot was raised and there were five callers to Cowboy in the big blind. He has A-Q and he throws it away because a queen is already gone. Now the flop comes A-A-Q!

They started off firing at this pot — Jesse Alto's drunk and bluffing like hell and he's getting called by two players. Rusty LePage is drinking and ol' Sam Moon's in there firing, he's stuck. And all the action would have been in front of Cowboy, coming into him. This pot had $60,000 in it if it had a penny. And Alto won it with two sevens — he caught a seven on the end!

I don't think Cowboy was ever the same after that one. That would've been $60,000 in his pocket. But once that queen gets burned you're playing short-decked, so you can't play the ace-queen. I didn't say a word, just got out of my chair and left — I knew that the steam had to be coming out of his ears and everywhere else. And I've never seen Cowboy play that high again.

Jesse could've had deuce-seven offsuit or something like that, for all I knew, instead of those pocket sevens. When he was drunk, his money was a giveaway. He'd play for two or three months and get a hold of a bankroll (he was never broke) and then get drunk one night and that whole bankroll went in that one game — it was gone. Jesse's wife Bertha had money and she'd loan it to him on a percentage — he had to pay her back a percentage on the money he borrowed from her just to get back in action.

Benny in the Good Ol' Days

Benny Binion was a piece of work. There are probably a thousand stories that could be told about Benny, but I don't know them all. In his younger days in Dallas he ran the dice games and other kinds of gambling. We used to sit around the Horseshoe in Benny's later years and eat breakfast at a big circular table behind the Sombrero Room and he'd tell us some of the stories about his gambling days back in Texas. He'd say, "You never worried about getting broke. If you got broke, you just went out and robbed the bootleggers." Just push a gun in a bootlegger's face, take his money, and you had a bankroll again. The bootleggers couldn't go to the cops because they were running an illegal business.

When Benny first came to the Horseshoe he never forgot his old compadres who had gone to jail for a little while here, a little while there. He knew that they wouldn't try to rob him because of his reputation, so he hired them all. When he first started, he had all those thieves working for him. He taught all of them and they all became great workers — and they were all pro-Benny. That's one of the reasons why the Horseshoe went over so big.

Natey Blank was an old loan-shark who had been connected a little bit in the old days. Benny had to take some money from Vegas to Reno and he was worried that Natey knew about it and was going to have him robbed. So he did the right thing: He hired Natey as a bodyguard to go up there with him. Benny was sharp. Just before he died, Natey used to hang out at the Aladdin when they were playing poker there. He was a Las Vegas character, a shylock, for a lot of years.

Benny treated his whole family great, had all of them working in the casino. Of course, there's been a lot of tragedy in that family, you know. First there was Barbara and now Teddy, they're both dead. Barbara had a problem with drugs.

We were sitting at breakfast one morning and Benny said, "Fellas, I just let it be known in the whole town that if I hear of one man selling one thing of dope to Barbara, he's a dead man." He tried everything to help her out, but she died from an overdose. I think she was the apple of his eye because he was always talking about her.

Benny helped more people in Vegas than anybody realizes. In the old days all the casinos banked their money on Friday and they'd keep a certain amount on hand. Well, Benny was always the cash place. If somebody put a big run on one of the casinos, they'd come down and borrow the money from Benny until the banks opened. The ones on the Strip would come downtown and get money from Benny or have the Horseshoe send money out to them so they could have the cash to pay off when somebody put a big hit on them. It didn't happen very often, but he always came through for everybody.

Benny liked to play poker but he wasn't a great player. And of course, it was his idea to get the World Series of Poker started. He started it off with very few people. They used to have that game over at the Fremont all the time with Tommy Abdul, who was a big bookmaker, and Billy Davis and Nick the Greek Dandolos. Nick was being backed by the Fremont at the time — you know he was a millionaire 77 times and broke again. They used to play real high razz over at the Fremont to let people see them playing. Those guys were all there and that's one reason why Benny started the World Series. He wanted to get all the best poker players in the world, put them in one spot, and see who was the best. That was his idea. He always had business in mind, too, so he put them on display. He loved poker.

But above everything else, his real passion was good food. Personally, I never liked his chili but they always called it "Benny Binion's Famous Chili." He had a ranch up in Montana, a big spread. All the beef that they served at the Horseshoe came off his ranch. Jack would run the World Series, but

Benny was the one who always made sure the food was right. When Benny was alive, the food was fabulous during the World Series. And he always had some oddball item in the line ... buffalo steaks, rattle snake, bear meat, or this or that. Every year they had some different thing, and they never had the same buffet twice during the entire World Series. I mean, the main courses were never repeated at any time. This was true all the time that Benny was alive.

Ken "Top Hat" Smith & Benny's Birthday Cake

There's a little story that came out of Benny's birthday party that involves Ken "Top Hat" Smith. You see, Ken has a top hat from the Ford Theater where Lincoln got shot. He always wore it in the big tournaments, and when he won a hand he'd stand up and doff his hat and say, "Whatta player, Smith! Whatta player!" Ken is one of the old-time gamblers around Dallas; he and Doyle have been buddies all their lives and are about the same age. Ken's well off money-wise, although his health is poor. And you've got to realize that Ken weighs over 400 pounds ... he's a huge man.

Just before this birthday party came up, he went on the Ultra Fast diet and went from 420 pounds down to 247 so that at the time of the party, he weighed less than I did at 252. On this diet all you get to "eat" is some canned powder stuff that you drink in milk-shake form. And you have to go to the Baylor clinic for counseling once or twice a week in conjunction with the diet, to be sure that you keep the weight off. Then after you've been on the diet for six or nine months, the people at Ultra Fast give you a three-month hiatus. After that three months is over, they put you on a different plan.

Ken was on this hiatus where he could eat some solid food so long as he just stayed away from fattening foods when Benny's birthday tribute came up. He and his wife, Elaine, and my wife Joy and I went together to the party. The eats were fantastic: The fella who used to be the head chef at the Horseshoe had arranged the menu and supervised all the food. Well, Ken took a plate of food that you couldn't believe — it looked like a mountain on top of one of those thin paper plates. And he ate every bit of it.

Then they broke out Benny's birthday cake. It was a tall, three-tiered thing that was bigger than a wedding cake by a long shot. And Ken Smith went up there to get a slice of it — he asked for a big slice because he loves sweets and all that frosting and stuff — and he ate that piece of cake like it was nothing. You know how the frosting sticks to paper plates? He was running his finger around the edge to pick up the icing so he could lick it off his finger. I told Joy right then, "You can forget about the diet — he's never goin' back to it again." And today, Ken Smith weighs more than he did before he went on that diet ... after putting in all that time and strain.

Doyle Takes a Dinner Break

Several years ago during Amarillo Slim's tournament at Caersars, Doyle Brunson and I were playing at the same table. During the dinner break he went off and played some high-limit hold'em. When we resumed playing the tournament after the break, he leaned back in his chair and said, "If I can win the $51,000 they're giving away for first place, I'll only be $14,000 loser for the dinner break!" ♣

GLOSSARY OF POKER TERMS

Backdoor a flush/straight

Make a hand that you were not originally drawing to by catching favorable cards on later streets. "In Omaha there are so many *backdoor* possibilities that are unseen. A lot of times, you'll raise the pot with a hand like A-A-10-9 and you'll wind up winning the pot with a straight, not the aces."

Backup

A card that provides you with an extra out. "If you have a drawing hand, you should have a *backup* to your draw, a secondary draw. You always want an extra low card in Omaha high-low to *back up* your ace-deuce."

Beat into the pot

When an opponents bets an inferior hand, you gladly push your chips into the pot. "When three clubs came on the flop, Slim moved in. I *beat him into the pot* with my flush — he had a 10-high flush, mine was higher."

Behind

Other players will have to act before you do. "So long as you're sitting *behind* the other players, you have the advantage of position."

Big flop

The flop comes with cards that greatly enhance the strength of your hand. "I caught a *big flop* that gave me the nut flush, a wheel, and a set."

Boss hand

A hand that is the best possible high hand. "When you have the *boss* high *hand*, you should bet it as aggressively as possible, especially if you think two low hands are out there."

Bully

Playing aggressively. "When I have a big stack in a tournament, I like being able to *bully* the entire table."

Change gears

Adjust your style of play from fast to slow, from loose to tight, from raising to calling, and so on. "When the cards quit coming his way, Will didn't *change gears*; instead, he kept on playing fast and lost his whole bankroll."

Cold call

Call a raise without having put an initial bet into the pot. "Bonetti raised, Hellmuth reraised, and I *cold called*."

Come over the top

Raise or reraise. "I raised it $2,000 and Sexton *came over the top* of me with $7,000."

Commit fully

Put in as many chips as necessary to play your hand to the river, even if they are your case chips. "If I think the odds are in my favor, I will *fully commit*."

Counterfeited

When your nut low hand gets demoted by cards on the board that duplicate your hole cards. "You should always have a third low card to help out against getting *counterfeited*."

Dangler

A fourth card that doesn't fit in with your other three cards. "K-Q-J-6, three high cards with a *dangler* — who the hell wants to play that kind of hand?! That dangler can put you in a world of misery."

Decision Hand

A hand that requires you to make a value judgment. "The great hands and the trash hands play themselves. It is the *decision hands* that will determine your profit at the end of the session, the day, the year. It is all of the marginal, in-between hands that are played with great ability that separate winners from losers."

Flat call

You call a bet without raising. "When he bet in to me, I just *flat called* to keep the players behind me from folding."

Flop to it

The flop enhances the value of your hand. "If you don't *flop to it*, you can get away from the hand."

Get away from it

Fold, usually what appeared to be a premium hand until an unfavorable flop negated its potential. "If you don't flop to the low, *get away from* it."

Get the right price

The pot odds are favorable enough for you to justify calling a bet or a raise with a drawing hand. "Since I was getting the *right price*, I called the bet with a wraparound."

Get full value

Bet, raise and reraise to manipulate the size of the pot so that you will win the maximum number of chips if you win the hand. "By raising on every round, I was able to get *full value* when my hand held up at the river."

Get there

You have made your hand. "When you *get there*, you might be able to start maximizing your bets."

Give them

You attribute a hand to your opponent(s). "When the flop comes with a pair and your opponent raises, what are you going to *give him*? A straight draw?!"

High wrap

Cards that will complete a straight, no matter what high card comes on the turn or river. "When the board came with a 5-9-10, I flopped the *high wrap* with my K-Q-J-10."

Inside wrap

The ranks of your cards are between the highest and lowest cards on the flop. "If the flop comes with A-10-4 and you have K-Q-J-9 in your hand, you have an *inside* wrap."

Isolate

You raise or reraise to limit the action to yourself and one opponent. "Suppose you have *isolated* an opponent in pot-limit Omaha and you know that he has aces. If you flop a wraparound, you might continue with the hand since you have only one person to beat."

Jammed pot

The pot has been raised the maximum number of times and may also be multiway. "You should pass with a weak hand if the pot has been *jammed* before it gets to you."

Key card

The one card that will make your hand a winner. "I knew that I needed to catch a deuce, the *key card* to my wheel draw."

Lay it down

Fold. "Many times, you can put enough pressure on the pot to blow everybody away and sometimes even get the raiser to *lay down* his hand."

Limp

Enter the pot by just calling rather than raising. "In Omaha high-low you might want to *limp in* from up front with a premium low hand such as A-2-4-5."

Limpers

Players who enter the pot for the minimum bet. "With three *limpers* in the pot, I thought that my pair of kings probably was the best hand."

Live cards

Cards that you need to improve your hand and which probably are still available to you. "When three players who I knew to be big-pair players entered the pot in front of me, I thought my middle connectors might still be *live* so I decided to play the hand."

Live one

A loose, inexperienced, or bad player. "Very seldom do you get a *live one*, a person who can't play at all, in the big games but it does happen sometimes."

Long call

Taking a long time to decide whether to call a bet. "When you're studying whether to call, making a *long call*, your opponents can get a read on you."

Low wrap

The cards in your hand will make a low straight if one other connecting low card hits the board. "When the 3-6-7 hit the board, I had the *low wrap* with my A-2-4-8."

Maine to Spain

When you can catch any card on either end of the flop cards, or one of your own cards, to make your hand. "Suppose the flops comes J-10-2 and you have K-Q-9-8. We call it *Maine to Spain* — that's a big *big* hand."

Make a move

Try to bluff. "When the board paired sixes, Max *made a move* at the pot. I thought he was bluffing but I had nothing to call him with."

Middle buster

An inside straight draw. "If the flop comes A-10-4 and you have the Q-J-10-8, you're not going to draw to the *middle buster*, try to catch the king."

Nit and Supernit

A very tight player and a supertight player. "The *nit* is a person who plays tight and takes no chances. The *supernit* will drive from one county to the other, win one pot, quit the game and drive home."

(the) Nut draw

You have a draw to the best possible hand. "When two clubs come on the board and you have the A♣ 4♣, you have the *nut* flush *draw*."

(the) Nuts

The best hand possible at the moment. "Remember that you can flop the *nuts* and lose it on the turn. That's why you sometimes lay down the nuts on the flop in pot-limit Omaha against any action."

Nutted up

When someone is playing very tight. "Jackson was so *nutted up* at the final table, I stole pot after pot from him."

Out (an)

A card that completes your hand. "Always try to have an extra *out*, a third low card to go with your ace, when you're drawing for the low end."

Overpair

You have a pair in your hand that is higher than the highest card showing on the board. "I flopped an *overpair*, but folded against the action in front of me."

Pay off

You call an opponent's bet at the river even though you think that he might have the best hand. "I decided to *pay him off* when the board paired at the river and he bet because I didn't think that he had made trips."

Peddling the nuts

Drawing to, playing and betting the nut hand. "Remember that 90 percent of the time in Omaha, players are *peddling the nuts*. They may not be peddling them in a heads-up situation, but in any multiway pot, somebody's drawing at the nuts if they don't already have it."

Piece of cheese

A hand that is a loser. "If you raise and get reraised, your trip threes are probably *a piece of cheese*, so be very careful when you flop bottom set."

Play back

Responding to an opponent's bet by either raising or reraising. "If a tight opponent *plays back* at you, you know he probably has the nuts."

Play from behind

Checking with the intent of check-raising when you have a big hand. "I knew that Kevin usually *played from behind* when he had a big hand, so when he checked, so did I."

Play fast

Aggressively betting a drawing hand to get full value for it if you make it. "Many players *play fast* in the early rounds of rebuy tournaments to try to build their stacks."

Play slow

The opposite of playing fast; waiting to see what develops before pushing a hand. "When you make the nut straight on the flop and there's a chance that the flush draw is out or possibly a set, why not play your hand *slow* to start with?"

Play with

Staying in the hand by betting calling, raising or reraising. "You should realize that in Omaha high-low, you're going to *get played with* most of the time because it's a limit-structure game and because of that, there usually are a lot of players in every pot."

Pure

Certain. "In limit poker it is almost 90 percent *pure* that anyone who has called a bet on the flop will also call a raise on the flop."

Put on the heat

Pressure your opponents with aggressive betting strategies to get the most value from your hand. "You might consider *putting on the heat* when your opponent is slightly conservative or when he has a short stack against your big stack."

Put them on (a hand)

You assign a value to your opponent's hand. "Using my instincts and the way he had played the hand, I *put Stanley on* the nut low."

Rag (or blank)

A board card that doesn't help you and appears not to have helped anyone else, either. "The flop came with A-2-3 and then a *rag*, the 9♠, hit on the turn."

Rag off

The river card doesn't help you. "Then it *ragged off* on the end and he was a gone goose for all his money."

Rainbow flop

The flop cards are three different suits. "I liked my straight draw when the flop came *rainbow* and nobody could have a flush draw against me."

Read the board

Understand the value of your hand in relation to the cards on the board. "If you *read the board* correctly, you often can tell by the action that you might get a fourth of the pot with your A-2."

Rock

A very conservative player who always waits for premium cards before he plays a hand. "Smith was playing like a *rock* so when she bet in to me, I knew she had me beat."

Run over

Playing aggressively in an attempt to control the other players. "If they're not trying to stop you from being a bully, then keep *running over them* until they do."

Rundown (hand)

A hand in which your cards are connected. "If it's a small *rundown hand* such as 6-5-4-3, the only time being suited comes into play is when you're heads up."

Runner-runner

Catch cards on the turn and river that make your hand a winner. "As it turns out, you had a suited K-J, caught runner-runner to make a flush, and broke me!"

Showdown

When no one bets at the river and the cards are turned over to determine the winner. "If everyone checks to you at the river and you couldn't win in a *showdown*, why bet if you know that you will get called?"

Scoop the pot

You win both the high and low ends of a pot in a split game. "The whole idea of Omaha high-low is to play hands that you can *scoop the pot* with."

Scooper

A hand that wins the whole pot. "When a third low card failed to come at the river, I had a *scooper*."

Slowplay

You intentionally do not bet a strong hand for maximum value because you are hoping to trap your opponents. "When pot-limit hold'em players move to pot-limit Omaha, they often make the mistake of using *slowplay* tactics to try to trap people. But you can't give free cards in Omaha — you don't *slowplay*, you play very straightforwardly. If you have it, you bet it."

Stand a raise

Call a raise. "I recently *stood a raise* in a cash game with 9-9-8-7. The board came 7-6-2, no suits. A guy led off with a decent bet and I called him with my overpair and straight draw."

Stiffed in

Play a blind hand in an unraised pot. "The only time you might play middle connectors in Omaha high-low is when you *stiffed in* in the big blind."

Smooth-call

Call a bet without raising. "If someone bets into you, you might *smooth call* with this type of hand because you have an extra out."

Take off a card

Call a bet on the flop. "I decided to *take off a card* and see what the turn would bring."

Takeoff hand

A hand that has the potential of beating a better starting hand because it is live. "In four-way action, I figured that my middle connectors might turn into a *takeoff hand*."

Take them off (a hand)
Beat a superior starting hand. "Any of those types of hands in which you have three rundown cards with a pair — will *take the aces right off* a lot of times."

Underbet
When you make a bet in no-limit or pot-limit that is considerably smaller than the maximum bet allowed. "You don't make a small bet to try to pick up a big pot. The *underbet* is a tip-off that you have a big hand."

Underpair
You hold a pair that is lower than a pair showing on the board. "Why would you ever want to call with an *underpair?*"

Outside Wrap
Connecting cards that will make a straight to the highest cards on the board. "If you have a K-Q-9-6 and the flop comes J-10-4, you have a three-card *outside* wrap.

Wake up with a hand
You are dealt a hand with winning potential. "Just because a player is a maniac doesn't mean that he can't *wake up with a hand.* Over the long haul, everybody gets the same number of good hands and bad hands."

Where you're at
You understand the value of your hand in relation to the other players' hands. "Your opponent may not know for sure *where you're at* in the hand when you have played it in a deceptive way."

World's fair
A big hand. "Suppose the flop comes 8-8-4, no suits. You know you're up against either nothing or *the world's fair.*"

Wraparound (Wrap)
The connectors in your hand wrap perfectly around the flop cards, giving you multiple ways to make a straight. "Suppose the flop comes 10-7-2 and you have J-9-8-6 in your hand. That's a complete *wrap* — you can catch a card on either end or in the middle and make your hand."

Cardsmith Publishing
The Championship Series

Championship No-Limit & Pot-Limit Hold'em
T. J. Cloutier and Tom McEvoy
Cloutier and McEvoy, two of the most famous poker tournament champions in the world, team up to bring you their best advice on how to win at big-bet poker. The champs show you how to win pot-limit cash games and no-limit and pot-limit tournaments. They teach you how much to bet, how to out-psych your opponents, and how to use position and chip power to win money at the world's most exciting poker games. Includes 30 pictorials of no-limit and pot-limit hands with 2002 Player of the Year Cloutier's expert commentary on how to play them in various situations. Written in a conversational style, the text is easy to read and understand. Includes stories recounted from Cloutier's colorful past as a road gambler. Foreword by Mansour Matloubi, 1990 World Champion of Poker. 212 pages, hand illustrations, photos, $39.95

Championship Hold'em
Tom McEvoy & T. J. Cloutier
Tom and T.J. give you their best advice on how to adjust to the new brand of hold'em with the latest strategies for wining limit hold'em cash games and tournaments. You will learn important adjustments in strategy to help you win more money in rammin'-jammin' games, kill-pot, bad-beat jackpot, shorthanded, and other types of cash games. The authors take you through the thinking process before the flop, on the flop, on the turn and at the river with specific suggestions for what to do when various things happen. Plus you'll get the inside scoop on limit hold'em tournament strategies that have led the authors to the winners' circle hundreds of times. 20 illustrated hands with play-by-play analyses and advice on how to make the most profit from them in cash games and tournaments. Includes a few of T.J.'s road stories, tips on playing hold'em variations such as high-low and a glossary. Foreword by Erik Seidel. Extensively revised and updated in 2002. 320 pages, hand illustrations, photos, $39.95

Tournament Poker

Tom McEvoy

Endorsed by World Series of Poker champions, this classic book outlines strategies for winning all the games at the WSOP. Revised and updated in 2001, Tournament Poker has been called the "bible" of tournament players. Extensive discussions of seven-card stud, limit hold'em, pot-limit and no-limit hold'em, Omaha, Omaha high-low, and 7-card stud/8-or-better. The 1983 World Champion of Poker also details techniques for winning rebuy tournaments, satellites, multi-game events, incremental rebuy and TEARS-structured tournaments. Includes insights into the ins and outs of big-league tournament play, how to negotiate deals at the final table, and answers to the most common questions players ask the champ. Revised and update in 2004. Foreword by Phil Hellmuth, 1989 World Champion of Poker. *"One of the most important poker books of all time."*— Gamblers Book Club. 344 pages, photos, $29.95

Championship Tournament Practice Hands

Tom McEvoy & T.J. Cloutier

This 2003 book gives you two types of instruction designed to help you become a winning tournament player. First, the authors let you get inside their heads as they think they way through the correct strategy for playing 57 limit and no-limit hands. These practice hands show you how world-class players use their skill and intuition to play strategic hands for maximum profit in various tournament scenarios, and give you specific how-to information. McEvoy and Cloutier also explain how 45 key hands were played by champions in turnaround situations at the World Series of Poker. By sharing their analysis and opinion about the way the winners and losers played these key hands, the authors believe that you will gain useful insights into how tournament poker is played at the highest level. Studying how champions think about and play major hands in challenging tournament situations will help you join them in the winners' circle far sooner than you ever imagined. Foreword by Dana Smith. 224 pages, hand illustrations, $29.95

Championship Satellite Strategy

Tom McEvoy & Brad Daugherty

Noel Furlong did it in 1999 for $1 million. Robert Varkonyi did it in 2002 for $2 million. Chris Moneymaker did it in 2003 for $2.5 million. Each of these World Champions turned a toothpick into a lumberyard by winning his way into the championship tournament at the World Series of Poker via a satellite victory. So can you if you follow the specific, proven strategies for winning satellites that World Champions Tom McEvoy and Brad Daugherty give you in this book. In addition to learning 10 Ways to Win a Set for the World Series of Poker and other major tournaments, you will find out how to win limit hold'em and no-limit hold'em one-table satellites for big-money tournaments, how to play supersatellites for the World Series of Poker, and how to win online one-talbe and multi-table satellites. The authors also include a special chapter on how to play poker's most exciting satellite game, no-limit hold'em. With the proven strategies that these two World Champions give up for you, you will be well armed to go to battle against world-class opponents in any type of satellite or tournament that you play. 208 pages, illustrated hands with analysis, photographs. $24.95

Poker Tournament Tips from the Pros

Shane Smith

As the popularity of poker tournaments escalates, this timely book gives you the winning advice of tournament champions, poker theorists and poker columnists on the best strategies for winning low-limit poker tournaments. Smith gives Top 21 Tips for winning tournaments and lists playing strategies for each of the Four Stages of Tournaments. Also includes 26 Tournament Traps and a Poker Potpourri of winning strategies. Smith documents the wisdom of poker luminaries Doyle Brunson, Tom McEvoy, Mike Caro, T.J. Cloutier, Bob Ciaffone and others. Especially designed for novice tournament players who want to move up the ladder. Revised, updated and expanded in 2001. 120 pages. $19.95

The Championship Table
(at the World Series of Poker, 1970-2002)
Dana Smith, Tom McEvoy & Ralph Wheeler
The Championship Table celebrates the poker players of the last three decades who have thrown theirs hats (and $10,000) into the ring in their quest to win poker's most coveted title, the World Championship of Poker. From 1970 when road gambler Johnny Moss was voted the best poker player in the world and received a silver cup as a memento, through 2002 when recreational player Robert Varkonyi defeated 630 hopefuls and received $2 million for his victory, The Championship Table gives you the names of all the players who made the final table, pictures the last hand the champion played against the runner-up, how he played his cards, and how much he won. The book also features interviews with many of the champions and runners-up, as well as interesting highlight from each Series, photographs of the champions, and quotes from many of them. A fascinating and invaluable resource book for World Series of Poker and gaming buffs. 176 pages, 78 photographs. $19.95

7-Card Stud (The Complete Course in Winning)
Roy West
Veteran Card Player columnist Roy West discusses the latest strategies for winning at $1-$4 spread-limit up to $10-$20 fixed-limit seven-card stud. The author's style is both informal and instructional as he outlines 42 Important Lessons on how to win in casino and home seven-card stud games. "Think of me as your favorite uncle, a professional poker player, who is sitting across the table teaching you how to win at poker," West says. Includes numerous thumbnail tips on poker strategy and psychology, and an in-depth analysis of correct strategies for third street through seventh street. Plus a strong chapter by World Series of Poker champion Tom McEvoy on how to win seven-card stud tournaments. This book has become the classic in its field. 160 pages, paperback. $24.95

Omaha High-Low: Play to Win with the Odds

Bill Boston

Why not play to win with the odds in your favor? If you want to make the best possible decisions about which starting hands to play, you need to know something about the chances that a hand has of winning the high end of the pot, the low end of it, and how often it is expected to scoop the whole pot. In this 2003 book you will find the odds for 5,278 Omaha high-low hands—including the 100 Best Hands, the 50 Worst Hands, the Three Omaha High-Low Bandits, and Trap Hands to Avoid. Using Wilson Software, the author spent more than a year running hand simulations and carefully documenting the results. With the assistance of Shane Smith, he has presented his research results and commentary in easy-to-understand language. 154 pages, paperback. $19.95

Omaha Hi-Lo Poker

Shane Smith

Geared to low-limit players who want to improve their game, Smith's 1994 book has become the standard on "How to Win at the Lower Limits," its subtitle. Smith outlines winning strategies for playing the flop, turn and river in ring games and Omaha high-low tournaments. Includes an in-depth discussion of starting hands and an odds chart. Also discusses lessons taken from live casino action with actual examples. "It's a gem!" — Lou Krieger book review in Card Player magazine. 84 pages, spiralbound. $17.95

You may order these books directly from Cardsmith Publishing, 4535 W. Sahara, #105, Las Vegas, NV, 89102.Our books are sold by Gamblers Book Club and Card Player magazine, plus gaming bookstores across the nation. Look for them on the web at Barnes&Noble.com and Amazon.com. For more information visit www.pokerbooks.com. Feel free to e-mail the authors at <author>@pokerbooks.com

T.J. Cloutier appeared on the cover of Card Player magazine in 2003 in recognition of his outstanding tournament achievements. Cloutier won the title of Player of the Year in both 2002 and 1998. You can reach the champion via e-mail by addressing your comments and questions to TJ@pokerbooks.com.

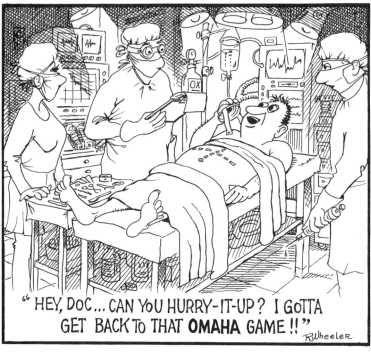

" HEY, DOC... CAN YOU HURRY-IT-UP ? I GOTTA GET BACK TO THAT **OMAHA** GAME !! "

R.Wheeler

from "The Wacky Side of Poker"
by Ralph E. Wheeler

"Pot-limit Omaha is the only game where you might fold the nuts on the flop and be correct in doing so." — T. J. Cloutier

"Omaha high-low was invented by a sadist and is played by masochists." — Shane Smith

"The players in the $3-$6 Omaha game were so bad I couldn't beat 'em!" — Numerous High-Limit Players

"Omaha high can be brutal! It's a cold, cruel world and it's a cold, cruel game ... but it's not as cold and cruel as Omaha split, which is even more aggravating! — Tom McEvoy